CYBERHEIST

The biggest financial threat facing American businesses since the meltdown of 2008

Stu Sjouwerman

CYBERHEIST

The biggest financial threat facing American businesses since the meltdown of 2008

Hi Jay!

Stu Sjouwerman

TechEd 2011

Publisher/Lead Author
Stu Sjouwerman

Contributing Authors
Naomi Alpern
Justin Korelc
Kim Lindros
Jeff T. Parker
James Pyles
Ed Tittel
Michelle Zavala

Developmental Editor
Kim Lindros

Copyeditor
Kitty Wilson

Technical Editor
Darril Gibson

Compositor and Graphic Artist
Kim Eoff

Proofreader
Kim Lindros

Indexer
Liz Cunningham

Cover Design
David Brier,
DBD International

Cover Art Photographer
Alan Poulson

Cover and Interior Printing and Binding
Globus Printing

CYBERHEIST: The biggest financial threat facing American businesses since the meltdown of 2008

Copyright © 2011 KnowBe4.

Trademarks

Trademarked names appear throughout this book. Rather than list the names and entities that own the trademarks or insert a trademark symbol with each mention of the trademarked name, the publisher states that it is using the names for editorial purposes only and to the benefit of the trademark owner, with no intention of infringing upon that trademark.

Warning and Disclaimer

Every effort has been made to make this book as complete and as accurate as possible, but no warranty of fitness is implied. The information provided is on an "as is" basis. The authors and the publisher shall have neither liability nor responsibility to any person or entity with respect to any loss or damages arising from the information contained in this book.

This book is also published in a variety of electronic formats. Some content that appears in print may not be available in electronic books.

KnowBe4
601 Cleveland Street
Suite 930
Clearwater, FL 33755
Toll Free: 855-KNOWBE4 (566-9234)
www.KnowBe4.com

ISBN: 978-0-9834000-0-4

Library of Congress Control Number: 2011904807

Published in North America by KnowBe4
10 9 8 7 6 5 4 3 2 1

This book is dedicated to all the sleepless cybercrime fighters in the world. You know who you are.
Thanks very much for what you do.

Acknowledgments

This project was a true team effort. My sincere thanks to all the people who helped bring my ideas to a tangible, cohesive book. This includes the following contributors: Naomi Alpern, Justin Korelc, Kim Lindros, Jeff T. Parker, James Pyles, Ed Tittel, and Michelle Zavala. Ed Tittel also designed and reviewed this book's entire contents.

The production team included these fine people: Kitty Wilson, copy editor; Darril Gibson, technical editor; Kim Eoff, layout design, compositor, and artist; Liz Cunningham, indexer; and Kim Lindros, who wore several hats, including proofreader and project manager. David Brier, DBD International, did the cover design, and the cover art photographer was Alan Poulson.

My sincere thanks to everyone who ever worked at Sunbelt Software and who helped to make us the Inc. 500 Success that we were. That was a great run!

About the Author

Stu Sjouwerman (pronounced "shower-man") has been in Information Technology for 30+ years, the last 9 of which were in IT Security. As a co-founder of Inc. 500 company Sunbelt Software, he has been specializing in antispyware products since 2003. A few years later, Sunbelt developed antivirus software, integrated a firewall, and at the same time developed antispam software for both consumers and enterprises. In 2010, Sunbelt was sold to GFI software, a portfolio company of Insight Partners, a $3 billion Boston-based hedge fund.

This is Stu's fourth book. He has co-authored three books about Windows system administration, the first being *Windows NT Power Toolkit*. Released in October 1999, this book reached #4 on Amazon.com's USA bestseller list the first week of its release and #1 in the UK. In 2003, a new book about Windows XP was published. The second and third books also reached Amazon's Top 10 List.

Since 1996, Stu has been the Editor-in-Chief of *WServerNews*, an email newsletter that goes to 100,000 IT system administrators and helps them to keep their systems secure, and up and running. Stu is now serving as publisher and editor of GFI Media Services, a division of GFI that produces four major online newsletters, including *WServerNews*, *WXPnews*, *Win7News*, and *GFISecurityNews*. These newsletters are tailored to deliver up-to-date technology information to both consumers and enterprises.

After having been on the software side of security, and still seeing workstations getting infected by malware, Stu realized that the human element of security was being neglected. He decided to start a new company called KnowBe4 that helps organizations train their employees to stay secure on the Internet. He lives in the Tampa Bay, Florida, area with his wife Rebecca and their three cats.

Table of Contents

Preface

The book you're holding, or viewing on a screen, is meant to educate you about the dangers of conducting business online. In particular, it covers several forms of phishing, a type of social engineering attack delivered over the Internet.

Our goal is to help you recognize the increasing danger that individuals and organizations face when they use the Internet, especially when conducting financial activity, and take proactive measures to protect your organization. These risks include theft of sensitive information, theft of goods and services, loss of intellectual property, and exposure to fraudulent online money transfers that empty your bank accounts: a cyberheist.

The dangers are real, and widespread. In the United States, losses to Internet crime exceeded $500 million in 2010, and these statistics are going up. Small to medium enterprises are particularly vulnerable to fraudulent wire transfers by organized cybercriminals. These crooks have become very skilled at social engineering and getting your organization's online banking credentials.

In addition, regulated organizations that handle private customer data must be even more vigilant. They face stiff legal and financial penalties if a thief breaches the data they store and manage. The fallout can cost an organization thousands to millions of dollars, ruin its reputation, and possibly shut it down.

Don't become a statistic. Read this book and apply the strategies and techniques described within to protect your organization from a potentially devastating cyberheist.

About This Book

This book consists of 19 chapters, divided into three parts.

Part 1, "The Business of Cybercrime," includes Chapters 1 through 8. In the early chapters, you learn about cybercrime attacks and techniques, and what drives attackers to create more and better scams. You also learn about phishing in particular, and several interesting variations on that theme. Part 1 continues with an analysis of how cybercrooks target certain victims (Chapter 6), and an overview of cybercrime losses and exposures (Chapter 7). It concludes with a detailed look at the percentages of cybercrime incidents in "Scary Reports and Statistics on Cybercrime" (Chapter 8).

Part 2 is entitled "Business Use Cases: Anatomy of Various Cyberheists" (Chapters 9 through 14). Each chapter tackles scams targeted toward a certain industry: banking, credit card and epayment processing, mortgages, banking clearinghouses, retail sales, and social networking. The chapters also explore scam scripts, attack methods, and protective strategies.

Part 3 of this book is called "Countering Cybercrime" (Chapters 15 through 19). It describes the fundamentals of safe computing (Chapter 15); how to integrate security policy, user training, and monitoring (Chapter 16); and how to protect people and assets with security technology (Chapter 17). You learn about online banking vulnerabilities in detail, and how to avoid them, in Chapter 18. Part 3 concludes with a discussion of how to raise Internet security awareness at work, and introduces the KnowBe4 training program (Chapter 19).

You can also find a list of acronyms and a glossary in Appendix A, resources in Appendix B, and references in Appendix C.

We use specific social networking companies such as Twitter and Facebook in examples in this book. Our intent is not to disparage these well-respected companies. Rather, we seek to point out the dangers that cybercriminals pose on these highly popular sites.

Special Elements Used in This Book

Throughout this book, you'll see a bomb icon here and there, and other text set off by bounding lines, italics, or shading. These are used to flag specific types of information and content. Here's a brief key to what you'll find:

- **Notes:** Additional technical or background information to help you understand attack techniques, Internet technology, or security tools and methods

- **Warnings:** Cautions about things to watch out for, avoid, or notice when working online

- **Cyberalerts:** Flagged with a bomb icon, this is information about cybercrime terms, tools, techniques and methods; often, definitions for specific types of cybercrime attacks

Contact Us

We'd like to hear from you with your comments, criticisms, and questions about this book. Please visit our website at *www.KnowBe4.com*, or email us at *cyberheist@knowbe4.com*.

The FAIL500 Project

Here at KnowBe4.com, as we began to assemble training materials for Internet security awareness and cybercrime prevention, we sat down and asked ourselves, what would the bad guys do to maximize their return on time and money they invest? After all, they think like businesspeople, too. So we also asked these questions: "What kind of companies would make the best targets for a cyberheist?" and "Why?" We realized that small but fast-growing businesses that focus primarily on rapid expansion and don't devote a lot of resources to IT security were probably prime targets. Where could we find such an exclusive group? The Inc. 500/5000 lists. (It wasn't that hard to come up with since I am an Inc. 500 alumnus; in 2001, my IT company, Sunbelt Software, made that list.) Better yet, the Inc. website listed the domain names for most of the targets.

Our plan came together in a few minutes. We would scrape the Inc. 500/5000 lists, build a database of domain names, use a free data-gathering service (aka an easily acquired hacking tool) to find all publicly available email addresses that belonged to each domain, and then send them a simulated phishing attack with no malicious payload to see which ones would be easy targets. We ran this by our lawyers and asked how we could do this without getting into trouble. They gave us some tips and said there would be some risks, but because this was a research project, they thought we could explain our way out of problems. They were right.

We scraped the Inc. site, gathering all the company names, locations, sectors of activity, revenues, and numbers of employees. Next, we deployed our data-gathering service and found about 40,000 email addresses for over 3,500 companies. Then, we ran a test using only 989 email addresses spread over 81 companies. We used an existing, high-reputation bulk email service to send this test batch, and let them know in advance what we were doing. We used a variant of a phishing email that required the recipient to click a link to indicate they were not spamming government servers. The email was sent by H.J. Granger, CPWP, CHP Compliance Manager, HSWW Government Services. You might recognize the sender's name and HSWW if you're a fan of children's science fiction/fantasy literature.

We had mixed feelings when we saw that, within a few hours, about **half** of all recipients at these random test companies clicked our link. The landing page we sent them to was a website created for this test at *www.phishingresearch.org*. On that landing page the recipients were notified they had taken part in phishing research and that all was well.

However, one alert soul reported us to the bulk email service we used (good for you!), and despite our earlier heads-up, that service suspended our account. We called to remind them that this was research, but a company rep said the test bruised the email service's reputation and that we had to find another solution. We agreed, and the account was turned back on. Next, we resorted to tactics that cybercriminals use for such attacks: we used a one-time mail server with an Internet Protocol (IP) address we were willing to put aside upon concluding the test, and sent our simulated phishing email to the rest of the 40,000 email addresses in our test pool.

Using an email server/IP address with an unknown reputation significantly reduced our delivery success rate, but we were still able to deliver some 28,243 emails. However, we were once again reported (excellent!), and our *phishingresearch.org* domain was shut down along with its hosting account. Delivery failure reports were still rolling in at the time we were shut down, so we were able to gather data for only about 21 hours in all.

The steps we took represented low-hanging fruit. If we had spent more time on each step we would have obtained significantly better results. We just wanted to know what percentage of the Inc. 500/5000 might be Phish-prone (that is, vulnerable to a simple phishing attack). This rate turned out to be 15%! Because there were nearly 500 companies in which employees clicked a link in a fairly transparent phishing attack, we decided to call them the FAIL500. The average number of employees per FAIL500 company was about 275, which means the companies are likely to keep significant funds in their operating accounts. No wonder cybercrime is a growth industry—cybercrime is easy, and the criminals would make the Inc. 500 themselves, with ease!

We then sliced and diced our data to determine the best targets (aka the most Phish-prone) by industry, size, location (state), revenues, and number of employees. The picture is not pretty. These are the top five Phish-prone industries: Travel 25%, Education 23%, Financial 22%, Government Services 21%, and IT Services 20% (you would think IT would know better!). It can take only one click to cause untold damage, loss of business, loss of cash, and massive legal bills.

Visit the *FAIL500.com* website to see the mind-numbing results. No individual company is singled out, although we gave a few people a call and suggested that they urgently give their employees KnowBe4 Internet Security Awareness Training! Whatever the ultimate outcome, we couldn't find a better demonstration of the need for such training, or the likelihood that phishing attacks continue to succeed.

Stu Sjouwerman and the KnowBe4 IT team

Part 1
The Business of Cybercrime

1

What Drives Cybercrime?

Willie Sutton was a famous twentieth-century bank robber falsely credited with answering the question "Why do you rob banks?" with "Because that's where the money is." This saying is so well known it's sometimes called "Sutton's Law." While Mr. Sutton never actually said this, it does explain the basic driver for cybercrime. An enormous number of people are active online, and thieves therefore turn to the Internet to find victims.

How many people are active online? Table 1-1 shows estimates for the global online population, by language, for 2010.

Table 1: Top 10 Internet User Populations, by Language

Position	Language	Internet Users
1	English	536,564,837
2	Chinese	444,948,013
3	Spanish	153,309,074
4	Japanese	99,143,700
5	Portuguese	82,548,200
6	German	75,158,584
7	Arabic	65,365,400
8	French	59,779,525
9	Russian	59,700,000
10	Korean	39,440,000

Source: http://www.internetworldstats.com/stats7.htm

The total for all these populations exceeds 1.6 billion users! However, Table 1-1 lists only the top 10 language populations on the Internet, so the total Internet population must be even bigger. It would probably be safe to add another 500 million Internet users to the preceding total for a rough guesstimate of 2.1 billion Internet users worldwide. Given a global population of 6.8 billion in 2010, that means just under one of every three people on the planet uses the Internet.

That's a huge pool of potential victims by any standard. All these users could be accessible to thieves using any working Internet connection. Because so many people who use the Internet also use credit cards, do their banking, and manage financial accounts online, it's no wonder that cybercrime is prevalent. It's also no mystery that cybercrime rates are going nowhere but up.

What Exactly Is Cybercrime?

One simple definition of **cybercrime**, or **cyberheist**, is "a crime whose commission involves a computer." A better definition for this book could be "a crime committed using an Internet-connected computer." This broad definition includes any kind of wrongdoing that involves interacting on the Internet. Thus, it covers massive email broadcasts (spam) that involve no other overt criminal activity. It also covers online postings involving libel, defamation, or hate speech, all of which are regarded as criminal in some jurisdictions.

The cybercrimes that are the focus of this book must be defined more narrowly. We want to dig deeply into various forms of criminal online activity. We are especially interested in attempts to acquire and misuse sensitive information, primarily to rack up ill-gotten gains. This means analyzing attacks or scams of many kinds. Some seek to obtain accounts and passwords for websites. Others attempt to gain access to people's online banking or financial services. Some involve theft of securities or commodities. Some seek to misuse credit cards without notification or permission. Ultimately, the cybercrimes that interest us most are those that supposedly also excited Mr. Sutton's interest in banks: These cybercrimes go after other people's money.

There's plenty of evidence that cybercrime occurs frequently, no matter how you measure such things. The Internet Crime Complaint Center (IC3) is a joint partnership between the US Federal Bureau of Investigation (FBI) and the National White Collar Crime Center (NW3C). The IC3 receives cybercrime complaints and reports statistics, acting as a central referral system for law enforcement and regulatory agencies. Table 1-2 provides information on complaints of cybercrime that the IC3 received from 2005 through 2010.

Table 1-2: IC3 Complaints Received 2005–2010

Year	Number of Complaints Received	Losses (in millions)
2010	303,809	Not yet available
2009	336,655	$559.70 M
2008	275,284	$265.00 M
2007	206,884	$239.09 M
2006	207,492	$198.44 M
2005	231,493	$183.12 M

Source: http://ic3report.nw3c.org/docs/2010_IC3_Report_02_10_11_low_res.pdf

As you can see from Table 1-2, hundreds of thousands of cybercrimes are committed annually, and the dollar volume of losses is increasing. Today, headlines regularly report enormous losses due to cybercrime. It's not unusual to read about millions of dollars being lost in a single heist.

In this book, we explore an interesting and disturbing trend: Businesses are bearing an ever-increasing portion of the impact of cybercrime. At the same time, large numbers of individuals are experiencing identity theft and related financial losses and ruined credit ratings.

Who's a Target for Cybercrime?

Historically, individuals have been the primary targets for cybercrime, and this is still the case. But with more people targeted at work, individuals who fall prey to cybercrime force their employers to suffer and absorb related losses. The short answer to the question "Who's a target for cybercrime?" is "Anybody with an email inbox or who surfs the Web." That's nearly everybody who uses the Internet, and you already know that's more than 2 billion people.

Let's look at an example. Consider a common phishing attack that targets financial professionals at small to medium enterprises (SMEs) (see Figure 1-1). An email arrives in Joe Biggs's inbox at example.com. It appears to originate from an Automated Clearing House (ACH) that processes payments for Mr. Biggs's employer. This message informs him that a payment problem is pending and that processing has been discontinued. Feeling some concern, Mr. Biggs reads further. Next, he learns that he must provide information about his company's account in order for processing to resume. He is asked to click a handy link in the message to provide that information ASAP, so that business can get back to normal. Sounds pretty routine, doesn't it? It's not.

Phishing

Phishing takes its inspiration from catching fish. Just as an angler uses a lure to entice fish to bite his hook, cybercriminals use hyperlinks to draw unsuspecting users to malicious websites. Phishing shares these things in common with its watery inspiration:

- It looks like an innocuous or even a legitimate email message, Tweet, or Facebook post.
- It seeks to get readers to provide information by responding to the message or clicking an embedded link.
- It often requests sensitive information about accounts, passwords, or identity.
- The hook gets "set" when a reader responds, even if only by clicking a link.

Security experts often label phishing as a kind of "social engineering." This term describes various techniques used to persuade users to part with information about themselves, credit card or bank information, and so forth. The idea is to glean something of value to enable theft. No nightcrawlers and lures are involved, but the victims often wind up gutted anyway.

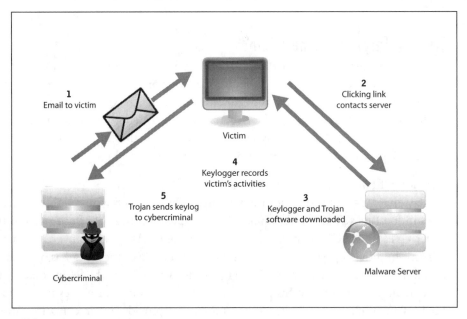

Figure 1-1
How malware gets from a website to a victim's PC.

If Mr. Biggs clicks that link, he is already at risk, even if he provides no information to the web page where that link takes him. That's because simply visiting a phishing page can expose a PC to software downloads. They occur in the background, covertly, without the user's knowledge or consent.

Cybercriminals who run phishing scams are especially fond of software packages like Zeus, which combine a keystroke logger (also called a keylogger) with a Trojan to harvest valuable information from unwitting PC users' machines. A keylogger records every keystroke that Mr. Biggs makes on his PC, and the Trojan periodically opens a backdoor to upload that keystroke log. The cyberthieves who planted this malware on his machine will comb that file carefully. They'll grab every account and password combination it contains, along with any sensitive data it might contain. If the bad guys can sniff out an online banking site and use Mr. Biggs's credentials to log in, they can transfer funds to other accounts right away. Talk about an unfortunate downside of 24/7 online banking services!

 ### Harvesting, and Malware

To harvest information means to acquire data illicitly. The data is usually some form of credentials, such as account names or numbers, passwords, and challenge-response sequences. An unauthorized third party—usually, a cyberthief—often uses the information to impersonate the individual or organization whose credentials have been stolen.

Malware is short for malicious software. Malware is any software that's installed on a computer with the intention of executing malicious code and/or causing damage. Typically, the software installs without the owner's permission.

If Mr. Biggs provides the information requested on the phishing web page, the thieves don't need to bother with a keylogger and Trojan software. They can simply try out the information he provided and see what it gets them.

"But wait!" you're probably thinking, "Does anybody really fall for this kind of thing?" A surprising number of people do fall for such scams. In fact, about one in five people in ordinary user populations fall for them.

KnowBe4.com has run surveys at various types of firms and observed success rates of 15% to 22% for its own simulated phishing attacks.

A January 2011 PCMag.com Security Watch blog article, "Phishing Effectiveness: 35 Credit Cards in 5 Hours," confirms this one-in-five ratio. This story reports how Internet security firm ESET discovered and monitored an obvious and crude phishing site in Latin America. The site was up and running for five hours on January 20,

2011. Of the 164 users who accessed the site, 35 users (about 21%) provided account information by filling out a form on the phishing page. This explains why online scams are so prevalent and why new variations keep popping up. Users keep falling for such scams, and these sites produce "free money" like clockwork!

A Million Stories for a Million Scams

Let's look at a quick sampling of warnings and reports of scams from the IC3 website:

- **Emails containing malware sent to businesses concerning their online job postings:** Companies download resumes and then become infected by malware payloads. The malware harvests sensitive data for transmission to cyberheisters. This is surely a sinister way to fight unemployment!

- **Fraudulent ACH transfers connected to malware and work-at-home scams:** Infected email attachments or drive-by downloads on malicious web pages harvest corporate banking credentials. This enables cybercrooks to access bank accounts and make fraudulent funds transfers. People seeking to generate income while working at home fall prey to account harvesting that costs them money instead.

- **Pop-up advertisements offering antivirus software:** Users respond to bogus virus discovery and repair offers to help them get rid of viruses they don't really have. These users waste money on worthless software. Worse, their machines fall prey to malware that can harvest sensitive data and cost them even more of their money. This software is called **rogueware**.

- **Fraudulent email claiming to be from the Department of Homeland Security and the FBI Counterterrorism Division:** Readers who download a purported speech by Osama bin Laden get malware instead. Thieves can then harvest and download sensitive data. Instead of keeping up with terrorism, readers get ripped off.

This list gives a good taste of the ingenuity and resourcefulness that cybercriminals bring to online scams.

Drive-by Downloads

A drive-by download is a transfer of software from a web server to an unsuspecting user's computer. It occurs in the background, with no notification, when a user visits a particular web page. It's called a "drive-by" download because a user need only access the page to be subject to the download. Such downloads usually include malware when some kind of scam or attack is under way. Such downloads can install themselves on the systems on which they take up residence, which means attackers can put specific types of malware of their choosing on victims' machines.

What kind of malware is in a typical drive-by download? Two items are common. The first is called a keylogger, which records every keypress a user makes on his or her machine into a special file called a keystroke log. The second is a class of software called Trojans, short for Trojan horses (after the famous ruse Greek warriors used to access the fortified city of Troy in *The Aeneid*). After a Trojan accesses a machine on the Internet, it ships a keylog to some recipient address. Cyberthieves comb this log for sensitive information. They're looking for accounts, passwords, and other information they can use to impersonate authorized users and steal their money.

Other phishing attacks recently reported from various sources include the following:

- **Attempts to collect bogus payday loans:** Disturbingly, these attacks feature lots of sensitive data about potential victims, including social security numbers, addresses, bank accounts, credit card balances, work history, and more.

- **Foreclosure-related scams:** Thieves use these scams to trick people in danger of losing their homes to waste their money on false remedies for their troubles.

- **Email account renewal scams:** These scams ask for credit card and other account information to cover a purported but nonexistent annual renewal fee.

- **Bank account and credit card information request scams:** Countless scams ask users to provide account details for hundreds of reasons, ranging from "database problems" to totally fabricated "security checks."

For every online account access or transaction where money changes hands, there's at least one scam that seeks to divert some of those funds into the wrong hands. For really popular forms of online financial activity, there are bound to be scads of such scams.

A Case of Criminal Culture

Criminals often learn their craft from other criminals, sometimes through direct contact and outright mentoring and sometimes through observation of what kind of crimes prove most successful. Cybercrime is a booming growth industry because it combines many characteristics that are especially appealing to criminals, including the following:

- **No physical risk:** Crime can be a dangerous business, particularly mugging and other forms of armed robbery. Cybercrime involves no direct contact with victims and hence poses no physical danger to its perpetrators.

- **No need for proximity:** Criminals must interact with their victims to commit their crimes. Working through the Internet lets criminals interact with potential victims from anywhere in the world, with no real-world contact needed, in a way that virtually guarantees preserving their anonymity.

- **A work-when-you-want schedule:** Sending email and putting up web pages require no real-time interaction with victims. A victim chooses to read an email or visit a web page whenever he or she wishes. The criminal need only check for resulting information harvests and be ready to act fast once potentially valuable information is available.

- **Tremendous opportunity:** The sheer size of the Internet user community lets criminals experiment with scams. They know they need to score with only a small number of emails or clicks to reap sometimes significant gains. It's easy to generate tens of thousands to millions of email messages, and it's also easy to post Tweets or Facebook pages to large audiences. Cybercriminals try all kinds of tricks to draw users to their malicious websites.

- **Small effort and big rewards:** Until the Internet came along, scamming required significant effort and finesse to generate earnings. It also involved physical risk and close proximity to victims. Modern criminals need invest only small amounts of time and effort to run Internet scams, but they can easily reap thousands of dollars in return.

Cybercrime is easy to do, involves little or no risk for criminals, and lets them work when and how they want, from any location in the world. If this sounds like an ideal job to you, think how it sounds to those with few scruples and a desire to make a quick-and-dirty buck.

Cybercrime Learning and Lore

There's more to cybercrime than ease, low risk, convenience, and payoffs. There's a learning curve to climb, and there's also a need to master the tools of the trade. Lots of successful scams breed imitation. Once a cybercrook learns how to run a scam, performing variations or refining targets involves little additional effort. Crooks can watch and learn easily from more experienced ones. After that, they can quickly get scams of their own going, too.

You already read about the Zeus toolkit, which combines a keylogger and a Trojan to make it easy to obtain and harvest accounts, passwords, and other sensitive information from unwary users. Zeus is just one of many toolkits that cybercriminals can use to package malware downloads that "phone home" to report on the user data they gather. For someone motivated by the illicit returns these tools can generate, spending a few days learning to use them is a modest investment for the "pot of gold" at the end of the road.

By watching others launch and manage scams, cybercriminals quickly learn how to scam. They formulate their own scam scripts, distribute emails (or Twitter feeds), and post web pages. Then they sit back and wait for results so they can take further action. This further action is likely to involve separating victims from their funds via unauthorized funds transfers, illicit credit card outlays, crooked epayment collections, and other methods of accessing account balances.

It takes only one or two trips around the block with a more experienced cybercrook for trainees to catch on and then start running scams for themselves.

Variations on a Scamming Theme

So far, we've explored a basic and simple scam: Create an email to provoke user action, harvest access information in response, and use that information to steal from victims. This takes little computing sophistication and is simple to implement. A scam appeal—be it email, Twitter feed, Facebook page, or whatever—is broadcast to as many addresses as possible, and cybercrooks sit back and wait for a response.

There are also elaborations on this scheme. In keeping with complex scams from the pre-Internet era, cyberthieves may research a specific group of victims. Then, they tailor a scam that's focused on and effective for a narrower audience. Thus, for example, ACH scams target financial or accounting professionals at SMEs. There's work involved in putting together a hit list, but professional association membership lists and websites, and even online phonebooks, make it easy to identify such people. These folks are most likely to handle electronic banking for companies where they work. Thus, they're most likely to have (or provide) the account information and passwords cyberthieves need to hijack those accounts and redirect funds as they please.

Even more sophisticated scams have been documented. After a particularly successful account harvest, a group of cyberthieves ran several electronic funds transfers against a victim company's accounts. At the same time, another group mounted a denial of service attack against the target company. The attack prevented the company's servers from accessing the Internet until after the first group transferred the ill-gotten funds. Because of the delay, automatic notifications didn't reach the intended recipients until it was too late to disallow those transfers.

Denial of Service (DoS) Attack

On the Internet, a denial of service (DoS) attack takes servers or networks out of play. Basically, such attacks involve overwhelming specific servers with so much traffic that they can't do their normal jobs. If a server is totally busy dealing with such an attack, it doesn't have the resources to do anything else. In the DoS attack just mentioned, cyberthieves drowned the servers with huge volumes of bogus network traffic. Those servers would normally issue fraud alerts to account holders and security personnel. All the bogus traffic bogged down the servers, preventing them from sending those alerts to the right people. In turn, this allowed other thieves to complete a series of funds transfers and siphon money out of the company's bank accounts.

Internet, and the Money Is Easy

The Federal Deposit Insurance Corporation (FDIC) protects individual citizens' accounts against theft and fraud. However, the FDIC doesn't protect corporate and commercial accounts in the United States—nor do other government bodies in the rest of the world. Also, business accounts tend to accumulate much larger balances than do personal accounts. FDIC insurance is limited to $250,000 per depositor per insured bank, but corporate balances often exceed this limit substantially. They are therefore valuable targets for cyberthieves.

A surprising number of SMEs, including school boards, municipal authorities, fire and police departments, and so forth, do not purchase fraud and theft insurance. Any organization without such coverage is responsible for losses if they fall victim to online fraud.

Once a cyberthief gains access to an online bank account, he or she often changes the account settings to enable money transfers to other accounts. Favored techniques here include authorizing electronic funds transfers (EFTs) where such transfers are not already authorized. Sometimes a cyberthief authorizes international funds transfers when existing account settings may only permit funds to be transferred to other US banks.

Favorite offshore transfer destinations for cyberthieves include Bulgaria, Romania, the Ukraine, the Baltic Republics, Russia, and Nigeria, among others.

Sometimes cybercrooks transfer money multiple times, in an effort to lose the wire trail from the source to the ultimate destination. In such cases, the crooks may open temporary accounts just to receive stolen funds. Someone will close those accounts once the funds move closer to their ultimate recipients. Occasionally, cybercrooks recruit local confederates to set up accounts and receive and forward stolen funds. This further obscures the money trail that EFTs leave behind. Funds transfers may involve intermediate hops in countries with lenient banking laws and where depositor anonymity is favored over criminal prosecution and restitution of illicit gains.

Offshore Has Definite Virtues—and Vices

Many cyberthieves set up operations in countries where law enforcement for cybercrime is lax, lackadaisical, or simply absent. Some countries choose not to prosecute such acts. Their leaders perceive no "local harm" involved for operations that funnel hard currency inside their borders because a ready and steady cash flow can provide many fiscal benefits. Other countries may be subject to graft and corruption. They offer a safe haven to cybercriminals, as long as local authorities and power brokers get a "fair share" of the proceeds.

The Internet is mostly insensitive to location and geography. This makes committing cybercrime possible and often absurdly easy. Criminals just set up shop where their offenses are ignored, tolerated, or treated as a source of income. This also makes it difficult for law enforcement in the United States, the European Union, and other areas to track down and prosecute perpetrators. Even in these circumstances, the FBI and other law enforcement bodies sometimes mount long-term, sophisticated "sting-and-grab" operations. They snare and then capture particularly glaring offenders and try them in US courts. Once cybercriminals get into that system, things usually turn out much less happily for those found guilty.

Avoiding Exposure to Avoid Losses

The old saw goes, "An ounce of prevention is worth a pound of cure." Where cybercrime is concerned, users who avoid clicking email, Twitter, or Facebook links avoid the possibility of drive-by downloads that can infect their systems with malware. In turn, they skip the part where their accounts and passwords get harvested. That prevents cyberthieves from using their information to steal, either from individuals or business concerns.

The motto at KnowBe4.com is "Think before you click." Savvy readers should internalize this motto for themselves as "I think before I click." If you don't click on a questionable link, there's simply no opportunity for a scam to succeed. Nor is there any way for cyberthieves to get their paws on your system or to harvest your accounts, passwords, and other sensitive data.

2

How and Why Scams Survive, Thrive, and Succeed

Fraud is the criminal act of misleading and misdirecting a victim through trickery. Computer fraud, or cyberscamming, is a multi-billion-dollar industry that affects people and organizations around the world. Money is a powerful motivator, attracting greedy criminals and victims alike.

As technology changes, criminals adapt their strategies to reach new victims. In the past, criminals used manual processes to scam victims: mailing letters, sending faxes, and dialing calls. Today, modern technology simply puts a new twist on old fraud schemes. Now the criminals use email and the Internet to reach their targets inexpensively and easily.

The global nature of the Internet works well for cybercriminals. They tend to work from countries with loose or nonexistent laws against online crime. A crook in Nigeria can target American victims via email; Romanian thieves can trap users through forged online bank sign-in pages; Mexican criminals can lure immigrants through text message spam. Most cybercriminals see online fraud as a nameless, faceless, fly-by-night crime that offers low risk and high reward.

In this chapter, you'll learn how and why scams thrive in the information age. Although victims of online fraud often lack security consciousness and online threat awareness, fraud isn't limited to the undereducated: smart, savvy people are also victims. Scammers succeed because they attack common human vulnerabilities: fear, honesty, greed, and gullibility.

The More You Try to Scam, the Better the Odds of Succeeding

Every scam is a numbers game. A scam may fail because the target won't cooperate for numerous reasons, including distrust, caution, intuition, apathy, or suspicion. To succeed, a scammer must exploit human vulnerabilities, and to find ideal victims the scammer has to cycle through large numbers of people. For every thousand emails sent out, a criminal may get only a handful of replies—but only one or two replies could yield hundreds or thousands of dollars.

Like an aggressive car salesperson, a typical con man is pushy and persistent. Not every customer is ready to buy a car, and not every recipient is a willing victim of online fraud. Both the salesperson and the scammer understand this, and their persistence increases the odds of success. The more often a cyberthief attempts fraud, the greater his or her chances of success.

The term **con man** *is an abbreviation for "confidence man," a swindler who gains a person's trust or confidence for the purpose of fraud. Once trust is gained, a fraudster can more easily take the victim's money.*

Persistence and Variety

Scams are fragile things: just a little doubt, suspicion, or common sense can alert a potential victim and foil the fraud. However, because the odds of earning easy money from an online scam are fairly high and scammers only need one individual to fall for the scam, cyberthieves have motivation to persist.

Variety is also important to a successful criminal enterprise. A single scammer can run several scams and reap big money. In one scam, she may commit wire transfer fraud; in another, she might harvest sensitive information through targeted emails; in a third scam, she could prey on purchasing department personnel through a phony business-to-business (B2B) website.

Another scammer might commit identity theft to perpetuate other schemes such as healthcare fraud. Persistence and variety are successful attributes for any scammer. Online scammers, like fishermen, cast wide nets in several choice places to catch a lot of what they're looking for.

A Successful Scam Spawns Countless Imitations

Bernard Madoff didn't invent the Ponzi scheme, but Madoff did master the method. For decades, Madoff defrauded investors of billions of dollars in his self-styled Ponzi scheme. Madoff's isn't the only Ponzi scheme to emerge in the past few years, but it is noteworthy.

Scams survive throughout time (often through variations) not because they're brilliant or clever feats but because an endless supply of people act as victims. In his book *The Big Con*, David W. Maurer writes of a saying among con artists: "There's a mark born every minute, and one to trim 'em and one to knock 'em." In other words, there's no shortage of victims (marks), crooks (those who scam others), and honest people (those who "knock," or warn others, of a scam or try to stop it).

Old Scams Finding New Victims

A quote often attributed to P.T. Barnum states, "There's a sucker born every minute." Even though Barnum didn't make up this idea, it's as true now as when it was decades ago. We might even add to it: ". . . and that sucker makes a fine target for fraud."

The following are just some examples of the variety of fraud currently in practice:

- Fraud involving online auctions and classified ads
- Phishing and smishing (that is, SMS phishing)
- Email chain letters
- Fictitious charities
- Bulk-mailing opportunities
- Work-from-home schemes
- Schemes that involve reducing credit card interest or debt
- Inheritance, laundering, and embezzlement scams
- Investment schemes such as pump-and-dump and scalping
- Ponzi schemes, pyramid schemes, and multilevel marketing
- Counterfeit money orders and cashier's checks
- Online automotive fraud
- PayPal and money transfer fraud
- Web service and credit card cramming (that is, billing for unauthorized services)
- Travel and vacation fraud
- Telephone solicitation fraud
- Health and life insurance fraud

The Internet exposes new generations to modern twists on old scams. Before email was common, fraudsters abused mail and telephone services to defraud individuals and companies. Fraudsters sent get-rich-quick schemes as chain letters to mailboxes all over America. In its basic form, chain letter fraud uses a list of names and addresses with a request for the recipient to send money to those people. In return, the victim's name and address is listed and circulated with the promise of exponential monetary gain. However, the financial benefit is actually earned by whoever orchestrates the scheme. Chain letter fraud persists in mail and email forms. Many victims are drawn to the prospect of a low-risk investment with high-yield potential.

For the record, any chain letter is illegal if it requests money (or any item of value) and promises substantial return for all participants. See Title 18, United States Code, Section 1302, the Postal Lottery Statute.

As another example, despite being a well-known Internet fraud, the Nigerian scam (also called the 419 scam) continues to operate three decades after it first appeared, but it now has many modern twists. It still finds its way onto lists of top scams published by organizations like PCWorld and PandaLabs. And according to Symantec, the Nigerian scam accounted for the largest number of fraudulent emails in January 2010.

The Spanish Prisoner is a con game from the 1800s in which the victim is told of a wealthy but unnamed prisoner in Spain raising money to secure release. In return for investing, the victim is promised a generous financial reward upon release—a reward that doesn't exist. Sound familiar? It should. Modern variations include advance-fee fraud, the black money scam, the Russian/Ukrainian scam, and the Nigerian or 419 scam. The Nigerian scam employs the same trick by promising financial gain in return for funds advanced. Dozens of variations exist throughout different countries.

Many modern scams are adapted from older schemes. Insurance scams are old, but criminals employ them in surprising new ways. Healthcare fraud costs US taxpayers over $60 billion a year. Medicare and Medicaid are defrauded in the millions; the single biggest Medicare theft exposed to date took $225 million. On the heels of US healthcare reform, senior citizens were being scammed by criminals preaching healthcare reform misinformation and peddling health insurance fraud.

Examples of Health Insurance Fraud

Health insurance fraud is big business. In May 2009, 11 members of New York's Bonanno crime family were accused of using stolen patient Medicare IDs to submit false claims. In another incident, Armenian criminals used stolen identities of doctors to establish 118 phantom clinics in 25 states to submit fake bills for bogus treatments.

Scammers are quick to capitalize on the irrationalities, fears, and knee-jerk reactions of desperate people, especially in uncertain times. State insurance regulators began to receive complaints about scammers selling "Obamacare" insurance policies in the wake of US healthcare reform. It's one of many tactics used to lure unsuspecting victims. Others include door-to-door sales of phony health insurance policies and useless medical discount cards. Obamacare insurance policies falsely claim that there's a limited open enrollment period to purchase insurance as required by law, preying on ignorance and fear.

Simple Technology Tricks Reap Major Results

Creating a web page is pretty simple. With some additional skill, many people can craft a convincing but bogus bank sign-in page or even a fake website that appears credible. A criminal with moderate coding skills can create, deploy, and remove a fraudulent site within minutes and vanish almost instantly.

Simple scams are easy to execute and deploy. Sending fake emails to capture personal details is trivial. Some are so poorly constructed that they contain warning signs: bad grammar, poor spelling, and suspicious uniform resource locators (URLs). Other scam emails are very convincing. A complex scam may involve multiple criminals in numerous countries, layers of secrecy, and varying explanations and excuses.

You'll see an example of an obvious email scam in Chapter 3, and another example that's highly believable in Chapter 4.

Insa Nolte, an African studies lecturer in the United Kingdom, says that email transformed local fraud into the Nigerian scam. The scam began in the 1980s, at the decline of a once oil-based Nigerian economy. Unemployed university students created a convincing letter that drew the attention of greedy business people wanting to make easy money. It spread to the West through letters and faxes, and then to entire companies. Copycat scams via email eventually appeared throughout Africa, Asia, Europe, and the Americas.

Trust Few, Share Little

Fraud can very easily be perpetrated via email and text messaging. New users of technology tend to be trusting, so issuing fake emails is a simple, low-risk way to generate quick results.

Customers often trust that only banks issue such statements and that only banks know their clients. People also trust text messages they receive from sources claiming to be banks and financial institutions. Subscribers often trust fake services they receive by cellphone, believing that only the real company would issue such requests. These are easy assumptions to make, but they cost people millions in ruined finances and credit repair every year.

Many people are also too trusting in what they reveal and share online to a mostly anonymous audience. Well-crafted search terms can uncover a wealth of personal information to help cybercrooks target victims.

How Technology Helps Fraud Schemes Evolve

Before email rose in popularity, most fraud was committed via mail and telephone. Charles Ponzi used the mail system in his famous scheme by taking advantage of foreign exchange rates. Nigerian scams were mostly local crimes until fax and telephone services spread them abroad. Email brings new life to old scams, as shown clearly with Ponzi schemes and Nigerian scams. Millions of nontechnical people use email, making them targets for fraudsters.

A Little Knowledge Is Indeed Very Dangerous

A little knowledge can be dangerous in the right circumstances. This statement cuts both ways: Knowing too little about online safety and security can be costly to victims in terms of damage to credit and credibility. On the other hand, a little insight into human nature often makes scammers successful.

For instance, humans are creatures of habit, and some are notoriously lazy. Many users choose passwords that favor convenience over security. For example, a typical user might use a weak password such as "password" or "123456" that is easy to remember and to type. Worse, some people compromise their own security by using the same password or similar passwords across multiple sites, including social networks, email accounts, and bank logins. Once a criminal obtains some credentials, he or she gains control over related assets. This can render significant damage and cause lifelong financial ruin to victims.

WARNING!

Efficiency helps accomplish a repetitive task with minimal effort, as when using weak passwords across sites. Weak passwords erode the strength of login security. If you reuse passwords, a criminal needs to uncover only one password to obtain all of your privileges. Even when a criminal does not target your accounts, he or she may guess your password while processing multiple accounts. For an eye-opener, see the list of the 500 worst passwords at *www.whatsmypass.com/the-top-500-worst-passwords-of-all-time*.

Taking Advantage of Human Nature and Gullibility

A swindler who commits fraud takes advantage of a victim through deceptive practices; the crook stands to gain personally or financially by stealing credit, identities, or finances. Fraud can affect just about anyone.

Fraudsters are students of human nature. They understand common thought processes, habits, and behaviors. They know how to manipulate emotional vulnerabilities to pull off all types of scams. Success at one scam builds criminal experience that leads to other scams.

Many scams are successful because many people are gullible. Scams work because people can be successfully tricked into revealing personal information, transferring money, or relinquishing control.

Some people remain gullible their entire lives; others eventually learn not to trust so freely. Finding a victim is simply a matter of cycling through groups of people to identify sufficiently vulnerable individuals to exploit.

Online scammers target all the popular places: social networks, job boards, auction sites, online classifieds, public forums, and everywhere else you go. Scammers know that such popular sites serve as major attractions that ensure a steady supply of potential victims.

To depict fraud victims as greedy, gullible, or stupid paints an inaccurate and incomplete picture. Even smart, well-balanced people are susceptible to fraud. Victims of Ponzi schemes are often honest, intelligent people made vulnerable through social and psychological factors. Social feedback—especially, word-of-mouth recommendations—plays an important role in the products and services people buy. When friends and coworkers share favorable or unfavorable experiences, their personal recommendations strongly influence the decisions of others around them.

Ponzi scheme victims are often bright people drawn to fraudulent investments by positive personal referrals from peers. And greed may not even be a factor. Friends of investors in Ponzi schemes are drawn to the sense of safety and excitement generated by strong social feedback. That's usually part of a scheme's design: Initial investors start small, get drawn further into the scheme, and unwittingly recruit other investors.

Anyone can be a victim of fraud, even an expert on gullibility or a well-informed investor. Sometimes scammers convince victims that they were specifically chosen for their honesty, integrity, or maturity. Because everyone is a potential target of fraud and because anyone can become a victim, there is no single personality profile that perfectly describes an ideal candidate for fraud.

Common Traits of Fraud Victims

Dr. Stephen Greenspan, a retired professor of psychiatry, wrote a book titled *Annals of Gullibility: Why We Get Duped and How to Avoid It*, based on his 10 years of research into why people fall for schemes and hoaxes. Dr. Greenspan claims that everybody is vulnerable in certain situations. Even smart professionals and savvy investors can be fooled by complex math, exaggerated returns, and manipulative pitches. Even so, factors that increase a person's fraud risk include the following:

- **Extroversion:** An overinflated sense of confidence with a tendency to wander outside one's comfort zone. Extroverts are engaging and interactive, socially approachable, and willing to share personal information with others.

- **Gullibility:** A willingness to skip personal evaluations in favor of good social feedback. Gullible people refuse to acknowledge their poor judgment or mistakes and prefer that others take control.

- **Risk tolerance:** A personal comfort level with different kinds of risk. High risk tolerance gives people a "thrill of the unknown," and all fraud schemes are high-risk proposals that promise unlikely financial rewards.

- **Blind trust:** A habit of readily trusting the opinions of peers or strangers without proper evaluation. Transference of trust breeds false confidence, which can deter a person from being cautious.

Fraud is one of many crimes scammers commit online and offline. This book discusses many different types of Internet-related crimes and how to protect yourself and your company from them. You'll learn how to recognize legitimate situations from bogus situations and get tips for avoiding problems.

It Really Can Happen to Anyone

Days after publishing *Annals of Gullibility*, Greenspan found himself the victim of Bernard Madoff's massive investment scheme, which he attributes to social feedback. By targeting groups, Ponzi schemers seek to manipulate the transfer of confidence to lure other victims. Charles Ponzi, after which the scheme is named, was an Italian immigrant, like most of his victims. Promises of safe investments combined with false confidence fool investors into letting down their guard. It's easy to see how even bright, cautious people fall prey to fraud.

3

Types and Methods of Attacks

While there are thousands of variations on the cyberheist theme, the number of attacks actually used to carry out online scams is much smaller than that. In this chapter, we will look more closely at the methods and mechanisms used to mount attacks for cyberheists. Along the way, we will also discuss how to avoid or deflect such attacks.

While reading this chapter, and when using the Internet, keep the following in mind:

- Always be wary when dealing with unexpected email or when presented with links to web pages that you know nothing about. In far too many cases, such emails are trying to trick you into visiting a website and providing information that you should not divulge.

- Remember that simply visiting certain web pages opens the possibility of a drive-by download that could install malware on your PC. This lets cyberthieves harvest information that you would otherwise not divulge.

The Social Side of Attacks

A phishing email delivers a carefully crafted message designed to get its readers to click the link it carries. Some phishing messages rely on explicit threats to force action. These warn readers of account inactivation or cancellation or threaten financial losses, extra charges, and so forth. Other messages seek to cause alarm by reporting unauthorized account access, unusual withdrawals, or suspicious account activity. Still others inform readers about unclaimed funds, unexpected winnings, or prize awards.

In many cases of phishing emails, the message tries to get readers to click a link. Readers see further requests for information on the web page that appears after they click the link. Unfortunately, it may already be too late to avoid trouble, even if the user immediately closes the page. What makes such access dangerous is that simply visiting the page can trigger a drive-by download (a malicious software download) to the user's PC, after which the software can collect all user keyboard activity and send it elsewhere across the Internet to a cyberthief.

You've Been Engineered ... Socially, That Is!

Social engineering is the term information security experts use for the act of talking somebody into divulging information that they shouldn't share with an unauthorized third party. Clever scammers rely on human impulses to be helpful, to avoid trouble or conflict, and to try to fix things when they break to extract information from unwitting and unwary users.

Social Engineering

The Encarta World English Dictionary defines social engineering as "gaining computer information by deception" as well as "the use of fraudulent means to gain access to computer systems that are protected by passwords or user IDs." Wikipedia, on the other hand, defines social engineering as "the act of manipulating people into performing actions or divulging confidential information, rather than by breaking in or using technical cracking techniques."

The key elements of social engineering reveal themselves in some of the words from those definitions: deception, fraudulent, and manipulating. Cyberthieves try to set up and define a situation where it will seem natural, normal, or helpful to provide the requested information or to click the link that's displayed. For non-email attacks, especially on social media such as Twitter or Facebook, all that's necessary is to present an attractive reason to get people to click a link. This, too, is social engineering.

The sections that follow take a closer look at some phishing attacks to show where the social engineering comes in. You'll get a chance to see how social engineering is designed to get a response from readers. Even if readers don't provide the requested information, clicking the link is good enough to give cyberthieves a "foot in the door."

Social Engineering Tools and Tricks

Cyberthieves rely on creating a sense of urgency in their victims. Phishing messages are designed to get victims upset, edgy, or anxious, so that they will respond immediately. Cool deliberation is nowhere in this picture—by design.

Many phishing messages start by presenting a situation and then explain the consequences of delay or inaction. Next, they present a link to fix that situation, and they often close by promising dire outcomes if the reader takes no action.

For example, consider this message purportedly from Google Gmail regarding unused accounts:

> Due to the congestion in the Gmail system, Gmail will shut down
> all unused accounts. You must confirm your email by filling out
> your login information below and then clicking the Reply button.
> Failure to do so will result in account suspension.

This message contains all the social engineering elements of a typical phishing attack:

- Account congestion and removal of unused accounts are cited as reasons for sending the email.
- Readers are instructed to confirm their email by filling out their login information.
- Readers are asked to click a Reply button (a hypertext link to the phishing site).
- Readers are informed that failure to comply with the request will result in account suspension and loss of access to their email.

It's easy to see that the cyberthieves are looking for account and login details. They play on the human tendency to be helpful and to help create order (for example, by reducing account congestion and getting rid of unused accounts). They give the reader no choice but to click the Reply button, threatening account suspension for a failure to comply. All this adds up to a calculated appeal to get readers to provide the information the cyberthieves want and to click the link.

Anatomy of a Blatant Phishing Attack

Email is the favored medium for phishing because it lets users click embedded links. Figure 3-1 shows a blatant and low-grade phishing attack. It further illustrates social engineering techniques used in related emails.

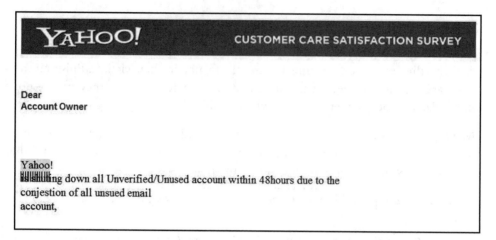

Figure 3-1
This snippet from a Hypertext Markup Language (HTML) phishing message shows all the ingredients of social engineering at work.

The remainder of the email message asks for personal information, such as user name, password, date of birth, occupation, and country of residence. The message sets up the urgency to provide the information by stating "Failure to comply means your Yahoo! email account will be deactivated without further notice."

Just the small snippet shown in Figure 3-1 contains a number of telltale signs of a phishing attempt:

- It's addressed to "Account Owner" rather than to an individual. Yahoo has sufficient information to address each recipient by name, and it would do so if it were the actual sender of such a message.

- There's a strange formatting error in the first paragraph of the message. The Yahoo! text graphic includes a shaded background with vertical strokes beneath that intrude on the text in that line. Likewise, odd line breaks follow after "Dear" and throughout the message body.

- The font used for the message salutation is very different from the font used for the message body (sans serif versus serif); Yahoo's own email messages use consistent fonts throughout.

- The message body text omits a space between "48" and "hours," and it misspells "shuting" (shutting), "conjestion" (congestion), and "unsued" (unused).

- The Yahoo! graphical header at the start of the snippet references a customer care satisfaction survey, but the message body isn't associated with a survey or attributed to customer care. Yahoo wouldn't do any of this.

In this message, the outright errors, formatting glitches, and strange mix of graphical and badly written textual elements point toward a phishing attempt.

Examining the Source Code

Now, let's take a quick look at the source code for the incoming HTML-formatted message. (To see it, you just click something like **View > Page Source** if reading email in a web browser.) Figure 3-2 shows a part of the message header from the phishing message shown in Figure 3-1.

```
X-YahooFilteredBulk: 82.132.130.169

Received-SPF: none (mta161.mail.sp2.yahoo.com: domain of
mailservice@yahoo.com does not designate permitted sender hosts)

Received-SPF: none(yahoo.com: yahoo.com does not designate permitted sender
hosts)

Received-SPF: DomainKey Not Present
```

Figure 3-2
A snippet from the message header shows that something is up!

Notice that the originating IP address for this message is 82.132.130.169. A quick trip to the *IP2Location.com* website reveals that this address is in the United Kingdom and comes from an Internet service provider (ISP) named O2 Online. If the message were legitimate, Yahoo would contact readers from the United States, and it would not originate its messages at a service provider that specializes in broadband and mobile phone accounts for consumers. (Yahoo uses Inktomi, as you'll see later in this section.)

The IP2Location.com website lets you know the physical location of the ISP associated with any URL through its IP address. You simply PING the domain name to get its address. (For a quick tutorial on the PING command, visit www.mediacollege.com/internet/troubleshooter/ping.html.)

Furthermore, the claimed Sender Policy Framework (SPF) identification is attributed to *mailservice@yahoo.com*, but Yahoo reports that it "does not designate permitted sender hosts." This means the claimed originator does not match the actual originator, and that the email address has been **spoofed**.

Further down in the message header, the text shown in Figure 3-3 appears. This text shows that the purported Message-ID, Reply-To, and From fields in the message as it displays in a web browser have all been faked. The less-than and greater-than symbols (< and >, respectively) make the enclosed text look as if the message originates from Yahoo, includes a Yahoo reply-to address, and comes from *mailservice@yahoo.com*, but all these entries are bogus.

```
Message-ID: <4C63A9A32EA52BFA@> (added by '')
Reply-To: <alertsevice25@yahoo.com.cn>
From: "Yahoo Service"<mailservice@yahoo.com>
```

Figure 3-3
These Message-ID, Reply-To, and From addresses are carefully faked.

Finally, there's a dead giveaway at the end of the message header (see Figure 3-4), where fields that begin with "X-SA" appear to indicate why this message has been flagged as spam. Spam Arrest, the spam-filtering service where we pick up some of our incoming email, labels the message a forgery.

```
X-SA-MPREASON: Forgery
```

Figure 3-4
The spam-filtering service detects that this message is a forgery.

Spam Arrest deduced the forgery from the mismatch between the actual point of origination (82.132.130.169) and the claimed point of origination (*mailservice@yahoo. com*). Yahoo's actual mail server address is 68.142.198.147; this real address appears in the email header for the Yahoo mail server that processed this message. IP2Location reports that 68.142.198.147 is in Sunnyvale, California, and operated by Inktomi Corporation for the domain name *yahoo-inc.com*, which is entirely legitimate—and different from the actual point of origination.

Spam

Spam is unsolicited and unwanted email, usually sent in bulk to thousands of email addresses. Spam emails generally try to perpetrate some type of scam or seek to verify live email addresses to which other spam may later be sent.

The Technical Side of Attacks

What happens when someone reading a phishing message clicks a link it contains? It doesn't matter if that link is in an email, in a Tweet, or on a Facebook or other web page. What matters is what happens when the user's web browser follows that link and opens the page on the user's desktop.

Disguise and Conquer

Chances are very good that when a phishing page opens in somebody's browser, it will be a convincing imitation of the website it claims to be. After all, anyone can grab the source code for any web page online, as well as the graphics that go with it, so it's trivial to create a web page that looks and feels much like the original.

Nevertheless, phishing sites often differ from the originals they imitate. As we saw for phishing emails, you'll notice occasional formatting glitches. Likewise, you'll see font or typeface mismatches. Sometimes odd combinations of headers and graphics will occur, as with the "Customer Care Satisfaction Survey" in the example shown in Figure 3-1. Noticing any of this requires a keen eye and a willingness to scrutinize small details. Many ordinary web users are oblivious to such details.

Hidden and Malicious Payloads

By the time a user gets to a phishing page, he or she may already be in trouble. That's because many such pages automatically install malware on any PCs that come to visit. These downloads occur without requesting user permission to proceed; in fact, they don't even inform users that they're occurring.

These downloads are called **drive-by downloads** because simply stopping by a web page causes them to occur. See Chapter 1 for a complete definition of this term.

In most cases, drive-by downloads rely on active content to work inside a web browser. **Active content** means that there's code inside one or more objects on a web page so that downloading the page can cause the code associated with such objects to be downloaded as well.

Active content comes in many forms. One popular type is ActiveX controls or applications, a Microsoft technology that's mostly associated with Internet Explorer. Another popular type is a Java applet, which requires a special browser add-in to work but is widely available for most web browsers. JavaScript (which is no relation to Java) is also popular for active content. Because JavaScript support is built directly into most web browsers, no other software is needed to let it do its work.

All these forms of active content—and more—can be used for both legitimate and safe applications and illegitimate and unsafe uses. Unfortunately, the shady variety is what usually takes up residence on PCs that visit phishing sites.

The Mechanics of Drive-by Downloads

When a browser downloads a page to a computer, it interprets the hidden instructions that govern how the web page is to be displayed. It also interprets and executes objects it finds referenced in those instructions. In general, this is how web pages handle active content. In particular, this is how the hidden instructions to download malicious active content can sometimes move onto a PC. If no anti-malware software is present to block viruses, spyware, and so forth, active content can execute freely. Even when anti-malware software is present, some malware can still get around a PC's defenses. When that happens, the malware installs itself on the visiting PC.

As mentioned in Chapter 1, two kinds of software are heavily favored for phishing attacks: keyloggers and Trojans. Keyloggers essentially install themselves as part of a computer's input/output system. They record all keystrokes that a user makes on the keyboard and write that information to a keylog file. If a user logs in to a website, accesses any online accounts, or enters credit card information on a PC with a resident keylogger, all that information goes into the keylog file. It will be of great and material interest to cyberthieves.

Trojans are special-purpose communications programs. They can use the Internet to establish backdoor connections to other machines and send them files and information. Used in tandem with a keylogger, a Trojan sends the keylog file to some designated recipient. When cyberthieves gain access to such data, they use it to make fraudulent bank transfers, misappropriate credit card funds, and do anything else they can think of to steal their victims' assets.

WARNING!

Another way thieves lure victims to rogue websites is by **tabnabbing**. Tabnabbing hijacks browser tabs, redirecting the user to fake login pages for online email, social networking, or banking or credit card accounts. Tabnabbing works when you have two or more tabs open in a web browser. When you leave a tab unattended for several minutes, a tabnabber can redirect the site in the unattended tab to a different, malicious login site.

Information Harvesting

Phishing attacks often include an outright appeal for information from victims. Think of the items requested in the Yahoo phishing attack cited earlier in this chapter: name, password, date of birth, occupation, and country of residence. Someone who provides that information is inviting identity theft as well as providing data about a specific email account.

Other phishing attacks are quite similar. ESET, a well-known Internet security and anti-malware company, detected an Internet phishing server at work. The company observed that 164 people visited a phishing site on January 20, 2011, in response to a classic account update phishing scam. Of the visitors who stopped by during the five hours the server was up, 35 of them (about 21%) provided all the information requested. This included personal information, contact data, credit card numbers, personal identification numbers (PINs), and more.

Though malware may be used to acquire and upload sensitive information to cyberthieves, it's not always necessary for them to go to such lengths to obtain it. In the ESET example, the average loss was $1,000 per victim, and 35 individuals experienced such a loss. That's a great return for a single short-lived Internet scam.

4

Phishing Explored and Explained

Phishing is a play on its sound-alike source word, *fishing*. The first recorded use of the term phishing appeared in 1996, when a team of hackers scammed AOL user names and passwords from unsuspecting users. These unwilling and unwitting pioneers received official-looking email messages that requested account information and gave a reasonable (but bogus) explanation for the request.

A surprising number of AOL users "bit" and provided their account information to the hackers. Various reports from that period say enough accounts were harvested to turn these "phish" into an unofficial currency among hackers. They would trade some number of phish for a piece of software or trade one group of phish for another, as they saw fit.

One of the earliest reports of phishing showed up in the media on March 16, 1997, in a story printed in the *Florida Times-Union* newspaper. It contained the line "The scam is called Phishing, as in fishing for your password, but spelled differently." Since then, Internet users have endured more than a decade of phishing attacks, mostly via email. In the past few years, however, the growth of social media such as Facebook and Twitter has prompted proliferation of phishing attacks via posting or Tweeting.

The Basic Laws of Phishing

When it comes to creating and maintaining user awareness of phishing, it's often helpful to break this form of criminal activity into its most basic components. A trio of terms captures just about every phishing attack we've ever encountered: imitate, motivate, and act (click a link, reply to an e-mail, or whatever). We therefore refer to these three actions as "the basic laws of phishing." The following sections spell out these laws in some detail.

Imitate

Imitation is the impersonation part of the phishing attack. An email phishing message strives to look like it comes from some particular organization. It may use the same fonts and the same logos to make itself appear legitimate. In short, many attackers try hard to make their messages look real and convincing. Sometimes the results are laughable, but other times they're very believable. However, even superficial examination of the header for such a message will show that the Sender (or From), Reply-To, and other standard email fields all point to impersonation.

Motivate

Motivation is the social engineering part of a phishing attack. A message may report that information has been lost or is missing; this type of message plays on a victim's desire to be helpful and solve problems. A message might inform its readers that an account will be canceled or suspended if they don't cough up the requested information; this type of message plays on the recipients' natural desires to protect their accounts or assets or to keep enjoying accounts and services that they like or want. A message might also indicate that until problems are addressed and information is provided, the victim can't use payment services or pay pending outstanding balances. Such instructions play on a reader's emotions, and seek to exploit human instincts to help others, avoid trouble, or fix things when they break.

All of these messages are sent for one purpose: to get readers to take action as requested in the message, Tweet, or Facebook post. All these threats, promises, and consequences are designed to provoke action from their readers so that attackers can obtain their confidential data.

Take Action Now!

The visible hook in a phishing attack is the form that users are requested to fill out. This is where they provide the details that cyberthieves are after to access their accounts and to steal or spend their money. To access this form, users must take action (click a link, send a reply, or whatever) in response to a phishing message, Facebook page, or Tweet.

An invisible hook may also lurk in a phishing attack. That is, the phishing page that a victim visits may cause a drive-by download of malware. If that happens, even users who don't bite the visible hook and fill out the form may still fall prey to the invisible hook if the malware download succeeds. The victim is then stuck with a keylogger and a backdoor Trojan that he or she may not know about for some time.

Fortunately, most users run some form of antivirus and antispyware software on their PCs nowadays. This should protect them from known forms of malware, but it may or may not protect them from new or unknown forms.

No PC is entirely safe from malware, so avoidance (don't reply to the email or click the link!) remains the best strategy.

Attack Anatomy 2: A Well-Done Phish

In Chapter 3, we analyzed a rude and crude phishing attack on one of our Yahoo email accounts in a section titled "Anatomy of a Blatant Phishing Attack." We deliberately showed a poorly done attack, to show that it's a wonder that some phishing attacks can succeed at all. Indeed, that particular example was rife with formatting errors and misspellings—obvious signs that the message couldn't possibly be legitimate.

In this section, we examine a more polished phishing attack message that uses the Federal Deposit Insurance Corporation's own logo and banner artwork (see Figure 4-1). It's nicely laid out and formatted, and it contains no misspellings—but it does contain two surprises. Only a few subtle grammatical errors provide telltale clues that all is not as it seems here. In the next sections, we inspect this ticking time bomb closely to explain its dangers.

The First Surprise: Steganography

The entire body of the message shown in Figure 4-1 is a single graphic. It is located on the blog page for a hosting provider's server based in Ireland (*webcore.ie*). Interestingly, this graphic appears nowhere in a blog on that server, and an Internet search on the graphic's file name (*fdic_finish1.gif*) turns up nothing useful. With no obvious connection to the message, something mysterious and probably illegitimate is going on here.

Further searching online turns up two examples of this message at the spam reporting site *spamigot.com*. Disturbingly, we used the jsunpack JavaScript Unpacker utility to analyze the image and found that the original image contains 22,349 hidden bytes

> Attention!
> Dear Depositor, this message was sent to you as you had indicated this e-mail address as a contact, by opening an account in your bank department.
>
> In order to inform you about the news concerning current business activity of the Company on a timely basis, please, look through the last important changes in current regulations of endowment insurance procedure. Please, refer to more detailed information in the attached document.
>
> Best regards,
> Federal Deposit Insurance Corporation
> Investors Relations Department

Figure 4-1
The message itself is only an image, but it contains two surprises.

of data out of a total of 36,981 bytes of content. In other words, only about one-third of the bits in this image are needed to paint the image on the screen, and the other two-thirds are unrelated and might possibly have sinister intent.

There's a word to describe what could be at work here: *steganography*. Fortunately, jsunpack reports that there are no "malicious or suspicious elements" in this particular image file, but there very well could be! Our guess is that a less-than-expert cyber-crook tried to craft a malicious payload inside the image but failed to create a working implementation. Nevertheless, the image certainly looks good, even if it doesn't work the way its creator may have wanted it to.

So, the first surprise in this phishing message is that the nicely crafted image that makes up the message body is carrying hidden freight. Fortunately, technical analysis of that freight shows that it contains nothing of a suspicious or malicious nature.

Steganography

Steganography has Greek roots that mean "covered writing." The Greeks sent secret messages between parties by covering up those messages so they couldn't be seen without removing an obscuring layer from the message. Today, steganography refers to the deliberate concealment of digital information within other seemingly harmless messages or digital objects, such as graphical images.

Steganography replaces useless or unused bits inside ordinary computer files with bits that make up some kind of message, information, or even executable code. The files in question may be graphics images, sound or video files, or HTML and other plain-text files. Even an encrypted file may use steganography, so that its secrets still lurk inside the content, even when encrypted content is successfully decrypted. A person needs special software to embed hidden information in a file, but the software is readily available. Many download sites offer usable and free steganography packages.

Unpacking steganographic content also requires software. Such software parses the altered file to pick out all the secret bits hidden inside its normal contents. Once unpacked, that content may be used in a variety of ways: to provide information, pass secrets, or even to run a program, possibly malware, that might have been disguised inside the carrier file.

The Second Surprise: A Malicious Attachment

The second surprise in the message is the attachment, as shown in Microsoft Outlook (see Figure 4-2). You can see that the ZIP file is only 317 bytes. Inspection of the ZIP file shows only a single empty directory named FDIC_Document, with no further content. Somewhere along the way, as the message made its way from its origination in Russia to the spam-filtering service in Seattle, Washington, someone or something stripped out its possible malicious content.

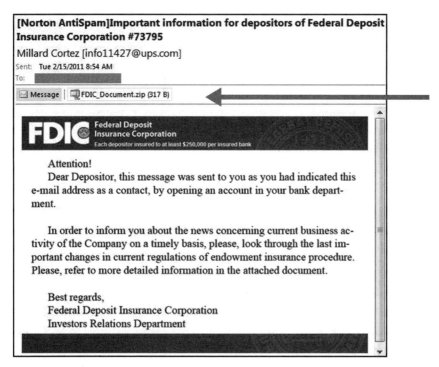

Figure 4-2
Outlook shows that this message comes with an attached ZIP file.

The spam-filtering service used in this example—Spam Arrest—might have removed a suspicious or recognizable malware file. Or automated screening at some other Simple Mail Transfer Protocol (SMTP) server might have done it sooner.

If this message had arrived the way its builders intended it to arrive, here's what would have happened:

1. The recipient would have opened the ZIP file to read the fake FDIC document in it.

2. That document would probably have contained a macro or some other active content that would have unpacked the steganographic content from the FDIC image. This content may have been the keylogger/backdoor Trojan combination that is typical of phishing attacks.

3. The software would have taken up silent and stealthy residence on the recipient's PC, harvesting keystrokes and sending them to a rogue server somewhere on the Internet in a few days or a week.

Telltale Signs in a Sophisticated Attack

Even the fairly well-polished attack we've been discussing has some telltale signs that should alert cautious readers that this email is neither legitimate nor trustworthy.

First, who is Millard Cortez, and why is he sending an email about FDIC regulation changes? It's also odd that the email address is so generic (info11427) and comes from the *ups.com* domain. This is a blunder from the senders, who should have spoofed some official address at *fdic.gov*.

Also, the message content addresses a generic recipient ("Dear Depositor") rather than an individual person—which is a strong sign of phishing. It's easier and faster to use a one-size-fits-all salutation than to do the work necessary to personalize each outgoing message. The entire message is overly stilted and formal and includes some small signs of originating from someone who is not a native speaker of English. In particular, the phrases "of endowment insurance procedure" (missing a "the"), the extra comma after the word "Please," and "Investors Relations" (should be Investor Relations) are all a little off-kilter.

The actual message header for this email, however, really shows the true colors and origins of the message. Figure 4-3 shows a text snippet from the SMTP transmission chain.

The supposed sending address for the message is 21.119.80.244, which is an arm of the US Department of Defense in Ohio. However, the actual sending address is 95.78.99.252, which turns out to be in the city of Naberezhnye Chelny in Tatarstan, one of the member states in the Russian Federation. This isn't a terribly likely point of origin for a message from the FDIC, is it?

```
Received: from dynamicip-99-78-95-252.pppoe.chelny.ertelecom.ru (un-
known [95.78.99.252])
    by mx2.spamarrest.com (Postfix) with ESMTP id 16A28C84E88
    for <ignatz@spamarrest.com>; Tue, 15 Feb 2011 08:54:11 -0600 (CST)
Received: from [21.119.80.244] (helo=wsspcniyhnbna.mfxfumcptnbazx.ru)
    by dynamicip-99-78-95-252.pppoe.chelny.ertelecom.ru with esmtpa
(Exim 4.69)
```

Figure 4-3
Part of the message header of the FDIC phishing email.

URL Shortening: The Good and Bad

URL shortening reduces the size and complexity of web uniform resource locators (URLs). It's designed to produce shorter strings. This is important in services such as Twitter, which limits Tweets to 140 characters. A single normal URL can easily consume most or all of those characters. In addition, long, complex URLs are not only difficult to remember, they're also challenging to enter manually (as when copying one from a hard-copy book or an article). Shortening uses a redirect service that provides a shorter replacement—usually under 20 characters long—for a long original URL.

Examples of services that provide shortened URLs are goo.gl, bit.ly, *and* TinyURL.com.

So far, URL shortening sounds like it's all good, but it can also be used to disguise URLs and prevent detection of known malicious sites or destinations. Instead of acting as a pointer to a website in Romania, the Ukraine, or Russia, a shortened URL link doesn't tell users much about where a link will take them or what they'll find when they get there. Phishing attackers love this!

Organization managers and IT personnel should warn employees to be wary when presented with shortened or abbreviated URLs. Most reputable shortening services offer preview options to show a fully expanded URL upon request. For example, you can install a preview plug-in for the Mozilla Firefox web browser that presents previews for any *bit.ly* link. You can preview TinyURL links by typing **preview** in front of a link string. For example, to preview *TinyURL.com/4c7ce7w,* you'd type **preview.TinyURL.com/4c7ce7w** (see Figure 4-4). TinyURL tells you that this shortened URL redirects to our own website, at *www.knowbe4.com* (see Figure 4-5).

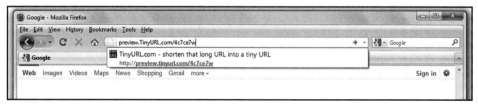

Figure 4-4
Previewing a shortened URL in Firefox.

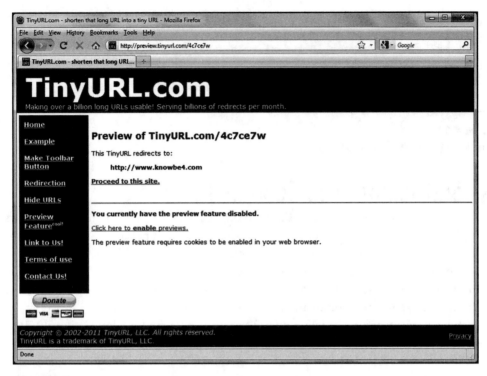

Figure 4-5
TinyURL indicates that the shortened URL is linked to the KnowBe4 website.

Surefire Ways to Avoid Phishing

First and foremost, the best ways to avoid falling prey to phishing attacks are to ignore spam and to steer clear of clicking links in Tweets, Facebook pages, suspicious blog posts, and the like. If that's too much to ask, be sure to look over messages, Tweets, and posts carefully, looking for the telltale signs of phishing discussed in this chapter. Above all, never respond to questionable emails or click the links in Tweets and posts. If you have a concern about an account or a financial transaction, directly visit the home page for your institution (*not* by clicking any link). Then either check your account online or use the organization's contact information to reach out to them by email or phone. If you initiate a conversation, that's one way to be sure scammers aren't involved!

5

Variations on the Phishing Theme: Smishing and Vishing

Phishing tricks victims, whether at home or in the workplace, into revealing private or sensitive data to an unknown party. Phishing attempts to fool victims into acting on bogus requests for personal or private data that only authorized parties should know. Typical phishing attacks occur over email and instant messages, but what began as computer fraud now also targets mobile phones and other wireless devices.

Because phishing is a form of social engineering, scammers try to appeal to a victim's sense of greed or fear, obedience to authority, social pressures, or trust in strangers. Phishing is an issue that affects people rather than technology, and it's unreasonable to expect software solutions to prevent all phishing attacks. Just as a weak password undermines the strongest authentication mechanism, uninformed choices undermine an individual's safety against social engineering.

Phishing has many derivatives and variations. In this chapter, we focus primarily on two interrelated types of phishing: smishing and vishing.

The Basic Mechanics of Phishing

Social engineering is a mind game. Social engineers play with human psychology to gain confidence and win confidential information. Cyberthieves use social engineering to realize a number of rewards: identity theft, financial fraud, or unauthorized access to protected systems.

Cyberthieves can apply manipulation techniques to many forms of communication because the underlying principles remain constant, regardless of the medium: Lure victims with bait and then catch them with hooks. Although most phishing attacks happen over computer networks, scammers are quick to target alternate channels. The same phishing principles apply whether an attack is via computer or by phone.

What Criminals Want from Victims

Though phishing can happen in various ways, the information that is stolen is typically numeric. The most valuable information includes the following:

- Credit card details
- Account numbers and personal identification numbers (PINs)
- Social security numbers
- Passport numbers
- User names and passwords
- Birthdays and anniversaries

Criminals use the data they harvest for identity theft and other forms of theft. Knowing birth dates and anniversaries can help them crack passwords or **challenge-response sequences** (questions) that sometimes serve as forms of authentication.

How Criminals Lure Victims

The fishing bait-and-hook analogy applies well to phishing. Scammers lure victims by using bait that targets specific social, mental, or emotional triggers. The phishing "lures" cybercriminals use to bait victims can take many forms, including the following:

- **Account suspension:** Threatening to suspend account access
- **Billing verification:** Requesting confirmation of or updated billing information, which is actually not needed
- **Unauthorized sign-in:** Warning that an account is locked because the number of attempts to log in exceeded a threshold
- **Software downloads:** Offering a free utility that will fix a computer problem
- **Lottery prizes:** Offering bogus winnings with processing fees

How Criminals Profit from Data Theft

Phishing is rarely a one-act crime. Usually it begins as a broader criminal strategy that involves various illegal activities, including stealing, selling, and otherwise misusing private or confidential information. A criminal who obtains social security numbers might obtain credit in the victims' names, buy goods online with that credit, and then sell those goods online or overseas. In the case of healthcare fraud, criminals may even sell stolen patient data to organizations that in turn use the data to defraud Medicaid and Medicare.

Criminals benefit from stolen information in the following ways:

- Using stolen identities for monetary gain
- Controlling the financial accounts of others
- Purchasing products and services
- Submitting phony credit and loan applications
- Pilfering funds, stocks, or securities
- Laundering ill-gotten money
- Stealing government benefits, such as social security checks and unemployment benefits

In many cases, committing the crime is easier than cleaning up the consequences. Criminals need only a few pieces of vital information and a little time to defraud entire groups of people at once. Victims, both individuals and companies, can spend years recovering from the damaging effects of crimes. It's no wonder criminals see phishing—and the variants we're about to discuss—as easy-entry, low-risk crimes that yield high financial returns.

Anatomy of a Smishing Attack

Smishing is phishing conducted via Short Message Service (SMS), a telephone-based text messaging service. A smishing text provides bait that attempts to entice a victim into revealing personal information; in this case, the hook is usually a uniform resource locator (URL) or a phone number. Attacks of this kind show scammers' versatility in reaching out to ensnare victims across different media.

For example, say that a credit union member receives a text message, warning that the member's account has been compromised and instructing the member to call a toll-free number. When the person calls the number, an automated system asks the person to enter his or her account number, PIN, password, or other private information. The criminal then uses this stolen information to perform identity theft. As another example of smishing, a text may urge users to install mobile antivirus software. When the person installs the software, he or she actually installs a virus instead. Such texts originate from infected PCs using computerized SMS gateways.

As discussed earlier, phishing draws on principles from social engineering. Those principles also apply to different media, including smishing.

You may see **smishing** *written as* **SMiShing** *to tie the term more closely to SMS.*

The strategy involved in smishing is ancient—it's just another form of Trojan trickery—but the delivery method is modern. Complex smishing attacks work in two stages to bait victims via phone and hook them via computer. Smishing may employ Trojan software or request private data to hook victims. Either way, the delivery methods remain the same.

Selecting the Bait

Bait texts create a false sense of urgency to encourage a victim to take action. Basic examples include unknown service charges, phony online purchases, cash prize winnings, and suspended account reactivation.

Setting the Hook

A smishing hook tries to entrap victims through solicitation and capture of sensitive information, or installation of malicious software. Hooks needn't be clever or complex to be effective. A person receives a text message that prompts an action. To gather information, the criminal might use dial-tone interpreters to decipher dial pad input, or speech interpreters to analyze speech. The action the victim takes usually involves the installation of a Trojan program.

A Smishing Example

Let's examine an example of a smishing attack:

1. The thief establishes a range of numbers to auto-dial. Even if only 1% of 1,000 people respond, the thief stands to gain quite a lot.
2. The thief creates a link to download fictitious security software. Once the hook is set, bait will lure the victims.
3. The thief sends a text message to a victim. The text urgently instructs the victim to download "necessary" security software.
4. The victim receives and reads the text message. The text message (bait) lures the victim to bite on the hook.
5. The victim complies with the instructions in the text message. The victim dials the callback number, installs the requested software, and is "hooked."

This attack could easily lead the victim to reveal private data to an automated system.

As shown in Figure 5-1, this smishing scam appeals to people with debt problems. This scammer makes an unusual request to reply by text. The real hook, however, is

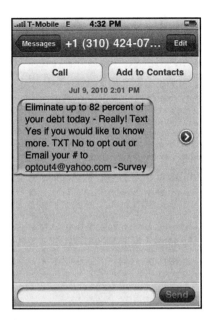

Figure 5-1
A blatant smishing attempt aimed at hooking people with debt problems.

the fake email address. If you reply, the scammer has your phone number and email address—as well as whatever follows through email correspondence. Everything about this text message—from content (debt elimination) to structure (SMS or email opt-out) to delivery (unsolicited message)—is questionable. But a trusting person with little security awareness may think nothing of responding to it.

Obvious attempts are easy to spot and avoid. Bad grammar, poor spelling, unsolicited messages, bogus URLs, forged emails, and shady get-rich-quick schemes are typical attempts. A well-crafted text at the right time can fool almost anyone. Anxiety, stress, fear, anger—emotions that erode our ability to think clearly and judge correctly—are excellent triggers for a scammer to exploit.

Anatomy of a Vishing Attack

Vishing is a phishing attack conducted by telephone, usually targeting voice over IP (VoIP) users, such as Skype users. Vishing exploits public trust in landline telephone services and is difficult for authorities to monitor and track. Scammers can fake caller ID data and hide behind bill-payer anonymity to dupe victims.

The popularity of vishing attacks has risen along with the popularity of VoIP services. Commercial and residential VoIP users are not required to provide valid caller ID data, which makes this technology ideal for committing fraud. Potential consequences of vishing include eavesdropping, unauthorized access to voicemail or billing information, voicemail overloading, and phone number harvesting.

Voicemail Overloading and Phone Number Harvesting

Voicemail overloading is also referred to as spamming over Internet telephony. Much like getting spam email, a VoIP user can get junk voicemails. Spammers simply send a voicemail message to thousands of IP addresses at a time. Because voicemail spamming is as easy as email spamming, a VoIP user can get a lot of junk voicemails quickly.

Phone number harvesting can refer to a few different things. Regarding cellphones, number harvesting occurs when users download free ring tones from a site that, in turn, uses the numbers to push advertising messages back to the phones. Number harvesting also describes a VoIP attack in which an attacker monitors incoming and outgoing calls on a VoIP system, building a database of phone numbers. The attacker uses the numbers to make unauthorized calls, for voicemail overloading, or for other deceptive purposes.

Selecting the Bait

Thieves may employ a number of phishing strategies to bait victims. All the emotional appeals, sense of urgency, and timing work exactly the same way as in other forms of phishing. What changes is mostly the delivery: In the case of vishing, voice-based telephony is the delivery system.

Setting the Hook

Vishing hooks may use callback numbers and automated recordings. Victims take the bait, dial the callback number, listen to the recording, and reveal sensitive information. Large-scale operations may employ an answering service or a call center unwittingly participating in the fraud. Hooking victims through vishing is nearly identical to hooking them in other forms of phishing; it's mainly the delivery mechanism that's different.

A Vishing Example

Let's examine an example of a vishing attack:

1. The thief uses a list of numbers stolen from a financial institution, a war-dialer to automatically call numbers, and a legitimate voice messaging service. The spoofed caller ID shows a legitimate organization name.

2. An automated recording alerts the consumer to the bait. The recording urges the victim to call a fake number for one of a variety of reasons, such as account expired, account overdrawn, fraudulent activity, billing errors, or whatever suits the scam.

3. The victim dials the provided number, which plays an automated recording. Voice instructions direct the victim to provide credit card or account numbers.

4.   The thief captures any other necessary details, such as security PINs, expiration dates, date of birth, and other important information.

For example, residents of Elgin, Texas, received automated calls from fraudsters claiming to represent KCT Credit Union and First Community Bank. In New York, recordings claimed to represent Cattaraugus County Bank and Mt. Vernon Money Management. In vishing attacks, sometimes the banks and credit unions are identified by name. Sometimes the callers pose as travel agents or lottery officials for unknown agencies. In every case, these callers offer only lies and deceit.

Vishing isn't limited to VoIP services with user-specified prefixes and identification. Third-party companies offer phone spoofing services, allowing callers to pay for anonymity. Some services provide VoIP for private branch exchange (PBX) systems, which connect the internal telephones of a private organization. These services also allow companies to select arbitrary phone numbers, and thieves use this situation to their advantage.

Why Smishing and Vishing Works

Vishing works because of technology convergence—that is, the merger of formerly separate and distinct technologies. Systems that were once isolated from each other can now interact with each other. Services that were once disjointed are now combined. Broadband phone services send calls over computer networks. The connection points to older phone networks create openings for criminals to commit phone fraud. Just as mobile banking services set the stage for smishing, VoIP extends phishing-like attacks to Internet telephony.

Broadband phone services allow users to acquire phone numbers with area codes in remote cities. Distant criminals can create the illusion of calling from local organizations. In some cases, intruders find ways around network defenses and actually do make calls from legitimate organizations. Proprietary VoIP protocols only worsen the problem by making it difficult for security experts to combat VoIP vishing.

Several other factors contribute to the success of vishing:

*   Inherent trust placed in telephone systems, especially compared to Internet messaging
*   A reachable phone-using population
*   General acceptance of automated phone systems
*   Common usage of overseas call centers with foreign callers
*   Flexibility of voice and text recognition
*   Tailored phone calls that seem more personal to the victim

IP telephony creates the opportunity for vishing attacks because of its social and technological reach. VoIP allows criminals to reach anyone, from any location in the world. Sending, receiving, and automating calls, as well as routing traffic through proxies involves minimal cost. Advanced vishing may use a malware agent to handle message delivery. An example of a malware agent is a botnet, which is a network of remotely controlled computers, usually meant for malicious purposes. (You'll learn about botnets in Chapter 10.)

Other Possible Variations Surely Lie Ahead

People buy hundreds of millions of smartphones every year, creating a rich market for scammers. As criminals turn to using text messages and VoIP to target victims, we can expect to see more fraud both at home and at work. We will see more worm, virus, spam, and smishing attacks against mobile users via SMS, mobile Internet, Bluetooth, and 802.11 Wi-Fi.

The following are a few of the emerging or increasing methods of smishing or vishing:

- **Mobile banking fraud:** As more people use their mobile phones to access online banking, fraudsters will target them with more realistic text messages that look like they're from the bank or credit union.

- **Mobile email downloads:** People will increasingly access their email accounts using smartphones, making it easier for thieves to download malicious software to the phones. Most phones don't have antivirus protection like PCs do, so detection is much more difficult for the user.

- **Fake access points (APs):** Bogus Wi-Fi networks look like legitimate shared hotspots in public places (such as airports, coffee shops, and hotels). When users log in or use these access points from their PCs or mobile phones, criminals capture all their data.

With new technologies rolling out every day, and as criminals experiment with these technologies, we will continue to see smishing and vishing scams adapt as well.

Avoidance Techniques to Live By

Because cellphone users are subject to smishing, mobile carriers must continually adapt their defenses to filter suspicious SMS texts, much like Internet service providers filter spam email. There's currently little recourse against many vishing scams, which may involve a single caller or an entire call center.

Common sense is a general best practice and should be an individual's first line of defense against online or phone fraud. Unfortunately, this is not always simple or obvious. Therefore, awareness training is a necessary line of defense against all online privacy and security threats.

Basic safety tips and best practices include the following:

- **Trust no one:** Even if you think a call or text originated from a legitimate institution, question the credibility of the source.

- **Know your numbers:** Call only trusted numbers, like those printed on billing statements or posted on official sites.

- **Hang up on uninformed callers:** Any caller representing a legitimate organization should know their customers and who they're calling, so hang up if asked for private or sensitive information.

- **Ignore and flag suspicious texts:** A legitimate organization enforces policies against alerting or communicating with customers via text messages.

- **Watch out for bogus pop-ups:** At a real site, a fake pop-up window may request sensitive information and appear to be part of the legitimate site. Use pop-up blockers to stop pop-ups from appearing in the first place.

- **Reveal nothing, conceal everything:** Provide no useful information to random callers. In fact, be cautious about revealing personal information to any caller. If you're asked for private or confidential information, insist on calling the company back using a number you know is legitimate.

- **Verify and validate:** If you receive an alert about account abuse or suspension, call the company directly and inquire about your account. Never use any contact number provided in an alert and always look up actual service numbers from bills or authentic websites.

As with any other online threat, with the various types of phishing, exercise good judgment. When it comes to fraud, you can never be too untrusting. Exercising too much trust is a weakness that creates victims out of just about anyone.

6

Targeted Scams: Spear Phishing, Whaling, and More

A great many phishing attacks look and feel much like ordinary spam. Emails, Tweets, and social network posts go out in volume. They simply target the general public—or at least anyone who actually reads the communication that starts the attack.

Not all phishing attacks are scatter-shot in their approach, however. Certain types of phishing schemes have quite a bit of focus. The attackers research a target population or a set of targets. These phishing attacks may not be as specific as wire and insurance frauds in the mid-twentieth century, but the attacks target specific types of individuals—and sometimes even particular persons by email address.

The more focused a phishing attack, the more work is involved for the attacker. But focused attacks must at least yield the typical one-in-five success ratio discussed in Chapter 1. That is, one in five people who visit phishing sites must be supplying the requested information. Otherwise, why would cyberthieves go to the extra work of targeting their victims?

The benefits of a targeted attack can be more substantial than fleecing the general public. In targeted phishing attacks, cybercrooks are likely to target victims who are better-heeled than the general populace. A successful targeted phish is likely to produce more cash or other items of value for the extra effort involved.

When it comes to targeted phishing attacks, security experts distinguish between two types of attacks: spear phishing and whaling. Whereas spear phishing goes after specific types of targets, often by organizational affiliation, whaling goes after specific (usually substantial and presumably wealthy) targets by name and identity.

Spear Phishing and Whaling

General phishing attacks target populations with specific types of accounts. These might be individuals with Yahoo or Gmail email accounts or individuals who bank at Wells Fargo or Citibank. Spear phishing aims to collect information about a specific organization or company. Spear-phishing messages may appear to originate from a large or well-known company or website such as eBay, PayPal, or LinkedIn. Sometimes in more customized attacks, messages that hit a user's inbox appear to come from a coworker or a member of the management team at the victim's own company.

Just as old-fashioned, seaborne whaling targeted the Leviathans of the deep, today's whaling attacks target high-ranking executives at major organizations or other highly visible public figures. These attacks are carefully aimed at specific individuals and feature all the details that legitimate email would also include. But because whaling is a kind of phishing attack, whaling messages create a sense of urgency or a need to respond in their recipients. They also provide a handy link for recipients to click. Once on a phishing site, victims are subject to drive-by downloads.

Let's take a look at the mechanisms of spear-phishing and whaling attacks.

Spear-Phishing Attacks

Spear-phishing attacks usually exploit publicly accessible company websites that offer contact information for employees and information about the target company or organization. Using details available from news stories, press releases, newsletters, and other sources, an attacker crafts an email message. This message appears to originate from someone inside the organization who has a right to ask for confidential information. It might be an HR secretary, a system administrator, a superior officer, or a first- or second-level manager in another department.

Spear phishers usually request user names and passwords, or ask victims to click a link that secretly installs drive-by downloads on their PCs. If one employee falls for this ploy, a spear phisher can impersonate that victim and start working his way up the food chain at the target organization. Ultimately, the spear phisher may hit pay dirt and obtain administrative passwords, bank account information, access to intellectual property, or other good stuff.

The occasional successes in spear phishing result from the organizational knowledge and details that attackers use to make themselves appear to be known and trustworthy. Information in a spear-phishing message looks legitimate, and the request seems valid. The recipients who fall for the ploy provide the requested details or visit the phishing site and fall prey to drive-by downloads.

Here's a dramatic example of successful spear phishing, as reported at *educause.edu* by security expert Aaron Ferguson. A person identified as "Colonel Robert Melville" who had a West Point email address sent out a spear-phishing message to cadets at West Point; 80% of them responded to this email.

At West Point, the prevailing e-mail culture is that any message that includes the rank COL (a military abbreviation for the rank "Colonel") in the salutation requires immediate attention. If such an email includes instructions or orders, cadets are to act upon them as directed. This particular email was a test rather than a real phishing attack, but it deliberately sought to exploit cadet culture, mindset, and training.

In fact, this email was actually sent by the West Point US Military Academy (USMA) Computer Emergency Response Team (CERT). According to Ferguson, the exercise tested the "security posture of the institution" and helped determine "the effectiveness of current security awareness, education, and training."

Students who clicked the link in the message were notified that they had been duped. They were also warned that their response could have resulted in the download of malware to their PCs. Given the high intelligence and caliber of the West Point Corps of Cadets, this example illustrates that well-crafted spear-phishing attacks can produce a higher-than-normal response rate. Whereas a typical rate seems to be one in five, this experiment produced a four-in-five response rate.

Whaling Attacks

Whaling attacks are usually quite sophisticated. In April 2008, the *New York Times* reported an attack that targeted thousands of high-ranking executives at financial services companies around the country. Each person received an email message presented as a subpoena from the US District Court in San Diego, California. Each message included the executive's name, company, address, and phone number and instructed its recipient to appear before a grand jury in an upcoming civil trial.

The handy message link in this case supposedly led recipients to a complete copy of the subpoena. But recipients who followed that link were subject to a drive-by download that included a keylogger and a backdoor Trojan. The *Times* story reported that "less than 40 percent of commercial antivirus programs were able to recognize and intercept the attack."

The particular attack reported in the *Times* was pervasive enough that two separate California federal courts, as well as the administrative offices of the US Courts, posted warnings on their websites. The attack prompted hundreds of calls daily to the courts identified. At the same time, antispam company MX Logic reported that it was observing 30 or more messages per hour matching this attack. More disturbingly, more than 2,000 victim PCs showed attack signatures indicating that the malware download had infected the target machines.

According to subsequent analysis of the attack profile and the malware involved, security experts linked this attack to an earlier assault that occurred in November 2007. In that case, the email message supposedly originated from the US Department of Justice and informed the recipient that a suit had been filed against his or her company.

Software installed on victim machines in the April 2008 attack communicated with a server in Singapore. The originator of the email appeared to have substantial knowledge of the workings and operations of the financial services industry in general. Various subtle clues in the message, however, suggested that the attackers were not intimately acquainted with the US court system. Other clues pointed to Britishisms, suggesting that the attackers might be based in Hong Kong or nearby in China.

This was a very carefully constructed and well-thought-out attack. But if the targeted executives had stopped to think, they would have immediately recognized it as a ruse. Why? Because a subpoena is an official court document. To be successfully delivered, a subpoena must be properly served. This requires filing a subpoena form, notarizing the subpoena, preparing and filing an affidavit of service, and delivering the documentation to a designated recipient in person. If necessary, a subpoena's server may be called upon to testify in court that the subpoena was served and to attest that all serving requirements were met. Email delivery is not an acceptable way to serve a subpoena!

Social Engineering Redux: Upping the Ante

The real dangers in spear phishing and whaling are the urgency and apparent validity of the messages. Spear-phishing attacks appear to come from trusted or well-known business partners, colleagues, or coworkers. Whaling attacks appear to originate from sources inside the legal, banking, or commercial communities that recipients know and work with regularly.

The West Point cadets example is particularly chilling. It illustrates that messages that appear to come from higher up in one's own chain of command not only invite a response but, in some sense, command one. You can also argue that the same logic applies to the whaling attack reported in the *Times*, where executives' inclination to comply with court orders and instructions was exploited to elicit immediate response.

When they succeed, both spear-phishing and whaling attacks are best understood as the triumph of social engineering over common sense. The plain fact is that clicking a link in an email message, in a Tweet, or on a Facebook page invites trouble. This is true even when the invitation to click appears to originate from a trusted source. Only when users realize that clicking a link carries a certain risk will they stop and ask "Should I click it or skip it?" In all cases, skipping it is the safest course of action. In most cases, a quick check of the uniform resource locator (URL) will reveal this to be so, so that's a good habit to cultivate any time you think you might actually be interested in what's supposedly at stake, on offer, or of interest.

Why Targeted Phishing and Whaling Attacks Succeed

One scary aspect of the West Point cadets example is that so many of the targeted recipients fell for this attack. We suspect that the same is true for other targeted phishing attacks. Certainly, the report in the *New York Times* that more than 2,000 executives' PCs were infected with malware from a single whaling attack suggests a higher-than-normal success rate. If thousands of executives were targeted and more than 2,000 machines visited the phishing site for the drive-by download, the minimum success rate was the one-in-five rate typical for ordinary phishing attacks. Unfortunately, it was probably higher than that.

The secret to the success of a targeted phishing attack appears to come from knowledge of the victim's world and surroundings. What makes these attacks compelling is their understanding of authority figures or agencies that can incite response. As explained earlier, this is a case of ingrained behavior trumping common sense. If an attack presents a convincing imitation of the victim's world and provides a good reason to get people to click a link, the attack has a chance of succeeding.

Unlike general phishing attacks, where victims may or may not be subject to drive-by downloads when they visit a phishing site, the probability of drive-by downloads increases in a targeted phishing situation. For spear phishing, it's probably a 50–50 proposition. For whaling, drive-by downloads approach certainty. That's because cyberthieves know that whaling targets have valuable information on their machines and desperately want to harvest it. With a chance to access such information, there's no point in asking such victims to supply confidential data. Besides, there's always a chance that asking for data would alert victims to the scam and prevent the attack from succeeding.

Anatomy of a Whaling Attack

The subpoena scam described earlier in this chapter is a good example of a well-crafted whaling attack. The scam message (see Figure 6-1) looks similar to a real subpoena (Figure 6-2). The originating email address, not shown here, includes an appropriate .gov domain. The link inside the message also looks legitimate, although a domain name lookup shows that it was registered in the United Kingdom, not in the United States.

Close attention to the differences between Figures 6-1 and 6-2 shows that the cyberthieves in this whaling attack didn't bother to download the latest civil subpoena forms from the Web (readily available at *www.uscourts.gov/uscourts/FormsAndFees/Forms/AO088.pdf*). There are obvious differences in layout and language. You can see the

---

AO 88(Rev.11/94) Subpoena in a Civil Case

_____

Issued by the

UNITED STATES DISTRICT COURT

_____

Issued to: XXXXXXXXXXXXXXXXXXX

COMPANY NAME HERE

COMPANY PHONE NUMBER HERE

SUBPOENA IN A CIVIL CASE

Case number: 91-201-NKE

United States District Court

YOU ARE HEREBY COMMANDED to appear and testify before the Grand Jury of the United States District Court at the place, date, and time specifiied below.

Figure 6-1
This mocked-up text from the whaling message described in this chapter looks somewhat like a real subpoena.

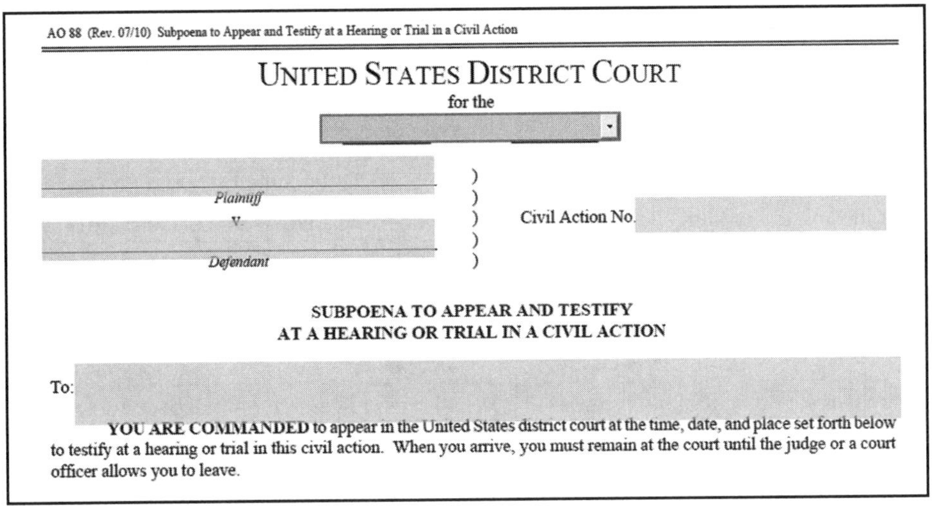
AO 88 (Rev. 07/10) Subpoena to Appear and Testify at a Hearing or Trial in a Civil Action

UNITED STATES DISTRICT COURT
for the

Plaintiff
v.
Defendant

Civil Action No.

SUBPOENA TO APPEAR AND TESTIFY
AT A HEARING OR TRIAL IN A CIVIL ACTION

To:

YOU ARE COMMANDED to appear in the United States district court at the time, date, and place set forth below to testify at a hearing or trial in this civil action. When you arrive, you must remain at the court until the judge or a court officer allows you to leave.

Figure 6-2
A portion of a PDF of a subpoena downloaded from the US Courts website.

various Britishisms cited in the *Times* story in the words "hereby," the language "appear and testify," and in mention of a Grand Jury (not relevant to civil cases in US courts).

However, for executives trained to respond quickly to court documents, this phishing attack was well constructed to elicit the response it sought: to get recipients to click the provided link. Though victims didn't see the full text of the subpoena, the drive-by download was already under way.

Spotting an Attack

Phishing scams—including spear-phishing and whaling attacks—end with a call to act, which usually means clicking a link. As soon as you spot a link you're supposed to visit in an email, in a Tweet, or on a social network page, you should be suspicious. Although there may be plenty of good reasons to click links in emails from parties you know and trust, responding to pleas, requests, or demands for immediate action is never advisable.

Table 6-1 compares the different kinds of lures that phishing attacks float in front of their intended victims with how legitimate interactions and requests normally work.

Table 6-1: Attack Lures Versus Legitimate Interactions

Attack Lure	Legitimate Interaction or Instruction
Click the link, or your email is suspended	Visit our website and consult your My Account settings
Click the link and collect your winnings	Notification occurs by mail, often registered
Click the link to read the subpoena	Subpoenas are served exclusively on paper
Click the link, or your account is frozen	Visit our website or call our customer service department
Click the link to download your update	Visit our website and use our download page
Click the link and access your grades	Log in to your student account online and check your current transcript

Note the common threads in the two columns. Phishing attacks ask, request, demand, or even command you to click a link. Legitimate instructions or interactions refer you to a website where you can log in to your own account or select information or downloads. Most such interactions also inform you that you may conduct business by telephone instead, if that's your preference.

If using the phone is your preferred way to conduct business, get the phone number from the company website or an online directory, not from an email message.

Some legitimate interactions, such as serving a subpoena, simply don't happen online. You might receive an email notification that you are to be issued a subpoena. But the subpoena itself will always be delivered in person, on paper, by a live human being. The same thing goes for sweepstakes, lottery, and contest winnings. While you may get a phone call, you will also be notified in writing for legal reasons. And when your winnings are delivered or deposited, you'll also get a visit from the IRS!

Surefire Spear-Phishing and Whaling Avoidance

We've said it before, we'll say it again, and we're saying it now: Don't click a link in an email, in a Tweet, or on a social networking web page. As the whaling attack details emphasize, clicking a link is all it takes to succumb to an attack. When cybercriminals take the time and expend the effort to mount a serious attack, the consequences can be serious. Think of the 2,000-plus PCs compromised by malware in the US district court subpoena whaling scam. And think of the heavy Internet traffic that was seeking to infect still more CEOs. Can you appreciate the clear and present dangers involved in whaling?

In general, if you want to manage an account, you should be the one to initiate contact with the institution involved. If you want to work online, that's okay: Just be sure to type or select the URL yourself and to make sure the padlock symbol shows up in your browser to let you know your connection is secure. (Chapter 15 covers Secure Sockets Layer, or SSL, and shows examples of the padlock icon that indicates SSL is keeping your Web communications safe.)

It also doesn't hurt to install good Internet security software, such as VIPRE Antivirus Business, and to make sure your software stays current and up to date. If you do much online banking, you might also want to visit the Trusteer website and download the Rapport anti-phishing software, too, to add an extra layer of protection against phishing attacks.

Must-Have Protection Software

You can download a 30-day trial of VIPRE Antivirus Business from *www.gfi.com*. This product provides speedy, low-impact protection against viruses, spyware, rootkits, and other threats. This package offers comprehensive endpoint malware protection with low system resource utilization, and it has earned both VB100 ranking and ICSA certification.

Trusteer Rapport is a browser add-in program that increases anti-phishing protection in most modern web browsers. It locks down web browsers, checks to make sure that websites use authentic current digital certificates, blocks drive-by downloads, and helps prevent online fraud. Download Trusteer Rapport from *www.trusteer.com*. (You will be asked to register with the site.) Set up a special user account on any computer you use for online banking and then log in to and use that account only when you need to do online banking. Rapport locks down your machine pretty tight and may otherwise interfere with your normal workday habits. If you set up an account only for online banking or other online financial activity, you'll want this protection. You'll learn more about Trusteer Rapport in Chapter 18.

7

Understanding Cybercrime Losses and Exposures

No matter where you turn for statistics on cybercrime, the numbers are big—and they keep getting bigger. As you read this chapter, remember that more than 2 billion people now use the Internet. Given a population this big, anything you measure is bound to be large, including cybercrime.

However, reporting and measuring losses is a tricky business. It's wise to treat such information with caution because crimes of all kinds tend to be under-reported. Thus, it pays to remember that no matter how bad things look, they could sometimes be worse. Exercising due diligence to minimize risk and exposure cannot be overhyped.

Cybercrime Reporting and Analysis

In his seminal book *The Natural Mind,* physician Andrew Weill suggests that philosophy and worldview exert incredible power over the ways humans perceive and interact with reality. He calls this viewpoint "What's in it for me?". It reflects the perspective of someone who's trying to make a case for some argument, or who wants to analyze a body of evidence to arrive at a set of "reasonable" conclusions.

Dr. Weill presents the idea that it's always wise to consider what axe a report or an analysis is seeking to grind. This perspective can be as important as the facts or information someone presents while reasoning through to some sort of conclusion or call to action. Perhaps restating Dr. Weill's maxim as "What's in it for them?" is more to the point.

Many cybercrime reports come from organizations that are in the business of reacting to and countering cybercrime. Remember that for an organization that neutralizes cybercrime threats or apprehends and convicts cybercriminals, presenting a bleak picture of the cybercrime situation can be very good for business (or funding, as the case may be).

Trends in Cybercrime

The FBI works in tandem with the National White Collar Crime Center (NW3C) to operate the Internet Crime Complaint Center (IC3). Its website (*www.ic3.gov*) is a clearinghouse for all kinds of information on Internet crime. The site publishes regular scam alerts as new cybercrimes are discovered and documented. The IC3 also publishes annual reports on cybercrime trends and activities. As we write this book, the most recent version of that report, *2010 Internet Crime Report*, is available at *www.ic3.gov/media/annualreport/2010_IC3Report.pdf*.

Some of the data from the IC3 report are so interesting and informative that we discuss them here. Let's examine some choice selections to understand the size of cybercrime losses, the volume of cybercrime activities, and references to cybercrime in online media.

Numbers of Internet Crime Complaints

Figure 7-1 shows a steady increase in complaints reported from 2000 through 2005, with a growth rate that varies from a high of 299% to a low of 11%. Reports dropped in 2006 and remained flat in 2007. Things picked up again in 2008 and 2009, but dipped by about 10 percent in 2010. The long-term trend, however, is clearly on the upswing.

While it's tempting to claim that complaints are steadily increasing, the data reported by the IC3 show a pattern of ups and downs. There's no doubt that the numbers have increased substantially from the beginning to the end of the reporting period (2000–2010), but the middle shows a slowdown in growth rate and a flat period from 2004 through 2007.

It's possible to see an inverse correlation with economic vitality in these data. The period 2000–2004 represents a rough economic patch, as does the period 2008–2009. The period 2005–2007, on the other hand, was relatively healthy and vigorous. There's really not enough data here to argue this as a statistically defensible conclusion, but the data is certainly quite suggestive.

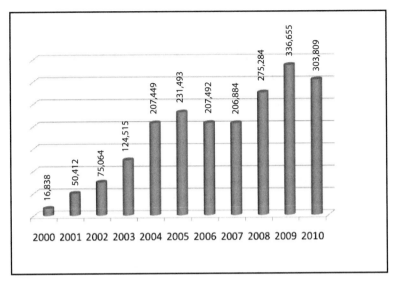

Figure 7-1
Annual number of complaints received by the IC3, 2000–2010.

For a different triangulation point, we can look to Google for year-specific searches for the period 2005–2010, as shown in Table 7-1. You can see some interesting patterns here, too, as you examine the results.

Table 7-1: Google Searches by Year on Cybercrime-Related Terms

Year	"Internet crime"	"Cybercrime"	"Internet theft"
2005	491,000	2,100,000	26,100
2006	549,000	2,520,000	32,500
2007	679,000	3,030,000	31,300
2008	770,000	3,690,000	32,600
2009	863,000	4,200,000	52,100
2010	1,130,000	5,800,000	58,500

Table 7-1 shows that reporting and coverage of cybercrime was on the upswing in the period 2005–2010. The "Internet theft" column shows the same wobble we see in the IC3 numbers for the period 2005–2007, suggesting that there is some correlation between complaints filed with the IC3 and reported to the media. This finding enhances the credibility of the IC3 annual reports, based on independent sources.

What can we conclude from this analysis? Two things jump out:

- Reporting and coverage of cybercrime has been steadily increasing over the past decade. It appears that this increase will continue for the foreseeable future.

- There appears to be a negative correlation between the general health of the economy and reported incidents of cybercrime.

Apparently, when the going gets rough, cybercriminals get going, too!

Losses Due to Cybertheft

Figure 7-2 shows losses as reported in the IC3 *2009 Internet Crime Report*. (The 2010 report omits a yearly loss report, so we show the data from the preceding year in Figure 7-2.) The graph shows a much steadier and smoother progression of losses from the past to the near-present, with two interesting outliers. The first is a nearly 50% dip in reported losses between 2003 and 2004, followed by a near tripling of that low-ball 2004 number going into 2005. This interesting dip in the curve precedes improved economic conditions that picked up again in 2005 and 2006.

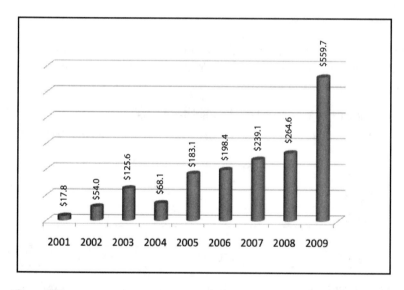

Figure 7-2
Annual dollar loss (in millions) of complaints referred to the IC3.

The second is a strong jump from 2008 to 2009, with losses more than doubling during that time. If our notion that an inverse correlation with economic health and vitality is correct, this indicates a strong increase in criminal appetites for Internet theft as the meltdown of 2008 gave way to the doldrums of 2009. Interestingly, IC3 didn't report losses for 2010, but the number of complaints for that year was down around 10% from 2009. Given that the economy also improved that year, if our inverse correlation holds, losses should also decline slightly for 2010 as well.

Notice also that we see only a gradual increase in the period 2005–2008 (a relatively healthy economic interval in the middle of that decade). This also seems to give credibility to our inverse economic health correlation. Whereas growth rates during tough times exceed 100% year over year, during better times, they appear to vary between a much smaller 8.3% and 20.5%, at least for the one period of record.

Two further observations are necessary. "Normal" cybercrime growth ranges from 8.3% to 20.5% are nothing to sneeze at. Plenty of legitimate organizations would be ecstatic about such growth rates. We also have to recognize that an inverse economic effect could also result from fewer individuals and organizations reporting Internet crime losses when times are good. When times are bad, losses tend to hurt more, so perhaps this is a more general effect of the economic principle that "a falling tide lowers all boats."

Chapter 8 digs into some of the IC3 statistics in more detail.

How Cybercrime Gets Monetized

The only cybercrimes that produce actual cash are those that raid bank or brokerage accounts or obtain cash advances from credit cards (usually limited to 20% or so of a card's credit ceiling). All other cybercrimes require selling goods or information to produce cash.

Not surprisingly, there's a thriving illicit economy where cybercriminals can trade ill-gained information or criminal services for cash. While reports on such exchanges represent only small and infrequent snapshots of this economy, they are interesting and show a thriving trading market at work.

Think back to the origin of phishing at AOL in the mid-1990s. Cybercrooks quickly began to trade "phish" for other things of value once the scam got going. Items traded included information about AOL accounts that could be used to impersonate a real account holder, steal his or her services, and make small purchases on somebody else's tab. Today's cybercrime market uses a combination of cash and barter, and it is basically an extension of the original "phish market," with many more items changing hands and a lot more cash involved. Table 7-2 lists some common items and describes the range of prices they can fetch on the cybercrime black market, according to Symantec and PandaLabs.

Table 7-2: Going Rates for Stolen Cyberinfo

Item	Symantec Estimates	Panda Labs Estimates
Bank account info	$15–850	$80–700
Credit card info	$1–30	$2–90
Email account login info	$1–20	N/A
Bank transfers and check cashing	50–60% of funds	10–40% of funds
Online stores and epay access	N/A	$80–1,500
Purchase/forward goods	N/A	$30–300 per item
Spam rental	$4–10 and up	$15 and up
SMTP rental		$20–40 for 90 days
VPN rental		$20 for 90 days
Web admin credentials	$2–60	N/A

The media is rife with stories about various kinds of web-based exchanges in such goods. You can look online and find reports on exchanges for stolen bank accounts and hijacked credit cards, for example. There's no question that a real underground economy is at work. In this economy, criminals with different skill sets are trading with each other to put together complete criminal operations, based on what they know and what others can contribute to their efforts.

A Terrible Spot for SMEs

The Federal Deposit Insurance Corporation (FDIC) insures bank accounts held by individuals for up to $250,000 each, but it extends no such protection to organizations. Larger enterprises typically pony up the cash to purchase cyber liability policies, or fraud insurance, so they obtain protection by spending money to hedge the risk. Small to medium enterprises (SMEs), on the other hand, normally don't purchase fraud protection. This makes them "self-insuring," in the language of the insurance industry—a rather polite way of saying that they must eat any fraud losses they incur. This is a tough situation. SMEs need to be aware of their exposure to fraud and perhaps to revisit their risk assessments. Who knows? Real fraud insurance may not be such a bad idea!

To make this situation worse, SMEs apparently can't rely on their banks to implement complete or reasonable protection against funds transfer fraud, either. Since 2005, at least three SMEs have brought lawsuits against banks, based on losses they incurred from fraudulent funds transfers. By and large, these suits charge that the banks involved violated section 4A-202 of the Uniform Commercial Code because they failed to provide "reasonable security" for that process.

Section 4A-202 of the Uniform Commercial Code deals with how banks issue and accept payment orders, including online funds transfers.

The Patco Example

A review of a summary of the allegations in the case between Maine-based construction company Patco and Ocean Bank is revealing. In *Patco Construction Company, Inc. v. People's United Bank d/b/a Ocean Bank*, Patco seeks to find its bank responsible for fraudulent funds transfers because the bank permitted multiple, larger-than-normal transfers to go through to offshore parties to which the firm had never transferred funds before. The allegations are also incredibly scary for what they say about the state of bank security and fraud protection for customers:

- The bank failed to offer or use security tokens or one-time keys to authenticate identity for online transfers.

- The bank used an unreasonably low trigger value to send challenge-response queries to users so that all transactions required challenge-response, and attackers were able to harvest all that data.

- The bank did not check the originating Internet Protocol (IP) address for transaction requests, nor did it block requests that originated from addresses not already approved.

- The bank did not detect transfer fraud, even though transfer amounts were larger than any prior transfers, went to accounts that had never before been used, originated from IP addresses outside the customer's networks, and occurred on days when Patco normally did not make funds transfers.

- The bank offered no dual control option that would require two individuals to log in to complete payment transactions.

- The bank established a transfer limit that exceeded Patco's needs, and allowed larger fraudulent transfers to go through.

- The bank failed to check Automated Clearing House (ACH) payment batches before submitting them for payment.

- The bank failed to send email alerts to Patco to alert them about unusual funds transfer requests.

This list is paraphrased from an article from the Information Law Group titled "Online Banking and 'Reasonable Security' Under the Law: Breaking New Ground?". The case is still in litigation as of this writing, but the outcome will be very interesting to banks and their SME customers everywhere.

The following are desirable features when selecting a bank with which to conduct online funds transfers:

- **Multi-factor authentication:** Insist that the bank offer multi-factor authentication to authorize funds transfers online. (Chapter 15 covers multi-factor authentication in detail.) If the bank won't purchase and distribute security tokens such as RSA SecurID or some equivalent, ask it to institute a practice of sending a one-time authorization key. This could come by fax to a prearranged phone number, by encrypted email, or by Short Message Service (SMS) to a cellphone available only to authorized personnel. (Given that RSA servers were hacked recently, asking for one-time authorization using one of the latter methods may be the more secure way to go.)

- **Regular frequent review of all transfers:** Insist that the bank review your normal funds transfer activity. Set any challenge question trigger value high enough to skip small routine transfers but catch those that exceed a threshold value you select in concert with the bank.

- **Confirmation procedures for large transfers:** Insist that the bank instigate confirmation procedures for funds transfers over some specified amount. In the Patco case, the initial fraudulent transfer was $20,000 higher than any single transfer made before. All subsequent fraudulent transfers were even larger than that!

- **Confirmation for unusual transfers:** Ask the bank to provide encrypted email or SMS confirmations for any unusual transfers that occur. Unusual might be defined as occurring on unusual days, for unusual amounts, and to new payees. The bank should hold all such transfers until approval is granted.

- **Acceptance of requests from only specified addresses:** Your organization can use IP blocking technology to register an IP address from which funds transfers may be ordered. The bank should then reject or require explicit telephone confirmation and approval for any alternate addresses from the account holder.

If any two of these stipulations had been met at the banks involved in lawsuits related to transfer fraud losses, none of those transfer requests would have succeeded. If banks won't police themselves, customers must force them to implement proper technical and procedural security measures. In the meantime, SMEs are on the hook for losses that might be incurred due to fraudulent funds transfers.

Reducing Phishing Risks

In a successful business-related phishing attack, a cybercrook may gain access to an organization's bank accounts. In this case, all funds on deposit are at risk. But this also means that a criminal can start changing account settings and security protocols. Such actions can facilitate transfer of funds offshore and delay fraud detection by the victim.

What does this mean? It means that, at a minimum, SMEs must contact their banks to understand current bank policies and procedures regarding account changes and online funds transfers. The best outcome of such a conversation would be to learn that no account policy changes can be implemented except under special circumstances. This might mean in person at a branch or in writing on company letterhead bearing the signature of a known and authorized company officer or representative. Such caution is seldom customary; however, customers should set up such agreements with their banks as soon as possible.

SMEs and other organizations also need to manage risks associated with possible financial losses resulting from fraudulent funds transfers. At a minimum, this means reviewing their banks' online funds transfer security practices and procedures. Organizations should also review their banks' fraud detection and notification capabilities. Then account holders must decide how to implement their own safeguards to further secure funds transfers online. One way to stop most fraudulent transfers is to require the bank to initiate a phone call to a designated contact person before allowing any online funds transfer.

In addition, the following steps can help you secure online bank transfers to reduce the possibility that a malware-based phishing attack could succeed:

1. Set up a separate user account on any machines where funds transfers are made. This account should then be used only for such transfers. Better yet, designate a specific machine to be used only for such transfers and for no other purpose.

2. Install anti-malware software (antivirus, antispyware, firewall, anti-rootkit, and so forth) on any machine used for funds transfers. Also install Trusteer Rapport on that machine to safeguard against phishing.

Chapters 6 and 18 discuss Trusteer Rapport and how to use it.

3. Establish a regular schedule for funds transfers (such as Tuesdays and Thursdays at 1 p.m.) and require prior confirmation with the bank via phone call or email to describe each transfer day's planned amounts and recipients. No call or email means no transfers that day.

4. Establish a list of regular recipients for funds transfers. Also establish maximum amounts allowed for each recipient. Financial staff and the bank should then carefully use these lists. All parties should question any off-list transfers or out-of-bounds amounts. The bank must get additional approvals (for example, from the finance department head, VP of finance, CFO, and so forth) before allowing such transfers to go through.

5. Finally, it's probably a good idea to meet with an insurance agent to discuss your online funds transfer activity and to learn more about the costs and benefits of fraud insurance. Cyber liability policies may not cost as much as you think. It's better to reject an option knowing its cost than to reject it out of hand.

Trends and Changes That Could Alter the Cybercrime Landscape

The outcome of the *Patco Construction Company, Inc. v. People's United Bank d/b/a Ocean Bank* case and other cases like it will have a profound impact on cybercrime. Given that SMEs—such as small businesses, school districts, tax offices, police and fire departments, and so forth—have been effective targets for fraudulent funds transfers, something must be done to stop these losses.

It's certain that the outcomes of legal cases will more clearly define the notion of "reasonable security" for online funds transfers. The definition that emerges from the legal process may require security measures such as those listed earlier in this chapter. Implementing such measures should drastically cut down on fraudulent funds transfers.

Financial prudence and a general desire to limit or avoid such losses will force banks to change their online funds transfer practices and procedures no matter what happens in these cases. But as long as organizations are responsible for protecting (and insuring) themselves against losses due to fraud, they, too, should take more steps to protect and secure their funds transfers against fraud.

8

Scary Reports and Statistics on Cybercrime

Cybercrime statistics serve many valuable purposes. One of the most important purposes is that they illustrate trends that drive responses and action. Cybercrime surveys are useful tools for identifying these trends and corresponding financial losses.

In this chapter, you'll learn that fraud encompasses all sorts of crime committed online and offline. You already know that fraudsters use computers and mobile phones to attract victims, target individuals and groups, and successfully hook many who should know better. Loss reports detail the financial and statistical impact of fraud as reported by survey participants. Unfortunately, the picture isn't complete because a majority of those losses are never reported.

Before we dive into loss statistics for recent years, let's take a look at some general organization-related cybercrime numbers for 2010 (from the Your Money Is Not Safe in the Bank! website):

- 55% of organizations reported incidents of fraud in the past 12 months.
- 80% of banks hadn't detected fraud before funds were transferred.
- Only 13% of fraudulent transactions were fully recovered.

Despite these sobering statistics, many small to medium enterprises (SMEs) believe the cost of fraud prevention isn't justified by the threats and potential losses. After all, criminals attack only big companies, right? Wrong. Although some criminals target specific individuals and groups, many cyberthieves cast wide nets and grab what they can. Depending on the scam, an SME is more likely to become a victim than a Fortune 500 company. It's in the numbers!

A joint survey by Visa and the National Cyber Security Alliance found that 85% of SMEs believe they are less of a target to cybercriminals than large organizations.

Loss Reporting Trends and Information

The importance of cybercrime statistics can't be overstated. While there are compromises to collecting and analyzing cybercrime, the results of surveys have far-reaching implications. Crime statistics aren't simply an academic exercise; they also drive public, corporate, and security policies. Best practices are often built around these numbers. Studies provide the benchmarks by which online crime is measured and defense budgets are weighed.

While you can't always compare study for study, you can draw reasonable conclusions from the results. Instead of focusing on dollars, you can compare cybercrime by percentages. Of all the participants in a survey, how many were victims of fraud? What are the top-ranking forms of fraud? Which types of fraud are increasing year over year? What are the emergent threats?

Statistics Don't Always Compare Apples to Apples

Always check the credibility of a source. That advice applies as much to online scams as it does to cybercrime statistics, which can be tricky for various reasons. Statistics may appear to tell a story, but they rarely reveal a complete picture, and despite the best intentions, they can be difficult to get right. Even when reliable studies from reputable sources are used, doubt may linger. Different companies often use different methods to analyze, classify, and calculate statistics, which makes it difficult to compare results directly.

Cybercrime statistics are especially challenging to analyze due to varying survey methods, different sample groups, and unreported losses. To make matters worse, consumers report crime only some of the time, and many institutions never file public reports. Financial institutions do report crimes to the Federal Deposit Insurance Corporation (FDIC) for analysis, but those details are never made public. The FDIC reports only performance statistics publicly; it doesn't disclose details of crimes.

Research methods also vary from study to study. Each survey involves specific selection criteria, uses idiosyncratic screening methods, and involves varying margins of error. Every study covers some specific time frame and sample group, but these time frames and groups seldom overlap or converge. Many classify and categorize the same crimes differently. The global nature of online fraud also makes investigation, prosecution, and analysis challenging. The upshot of all this is captured nicely in the title for this sidebar and is worth remembering as you read and digest cybercrime statistics in this book and elsewhere.

The Many Forms of Modern Fraud

Financial scams are vast and varied. Most studies focus on email scams, identity theft, and credit fraud—but these crimes hardly capture the full spectrum of possibilities. Scams constantly evolve to adapt to modern themes, such as the rise of "hitman scams" from would-be assassins to extort money from victims. (In a hitman scam, an alleged assassin extorts money through the threat of murder for hire.) The Internet provides a wealth of opportunity for fraudsters. It also provides access to millions of potential victims on which to practice endless variations on old scams. Tracking trends helps determine where criminals are focusing their attention and which groups are most susceptible.

Economic stimulus scams, healthcare reform scams, and online job scams all represent modern twists on old cons. Yet these are only a few of the emerging and explosive trends in Internet financial fraud. Playing on common fears, fraudsters have used economic crisis, healthcare laws, long-term unemployment, and trustworthy brands to defraud victims of billions over the past decade. Scams also adapt to new media such as social networks, text messages, and voice over Internet Protocol (VoIP) technology.

The Internet Crime Complaint Center (IC3) publishes studies based on victim complaints that span the spectrum of cybercrime. However, even the IC3 admits that its statistics are imperfect. Complaints are heavily influenced by consumer perception, which is often itself flawed, so two victims of the same crime might report it differently.

Conventional fraud is a vast and complex subject that's fraught with many challenges. The greatest problem related to categorizing and analyzing fraud comes from the number of variations on each scam. Consumers and organizations broadly define fraud as it overlaps schemes and technologies, such as smishing for identity theft to commit financial fraud. Confidence in trend analysis requires clean data from credible sources, and representative samples are only part of that picture.

Surveys are a primary source of cybercrime analysis. Companies such as Gartner publish reports on cybercrime statistics through surveys completed by consumers and organizations. In some cases, survey participants volunteer data through complaint forms, while in others individuals take more traditional fill-out-the-form surveys. In all instances, sample groups and sizes vary among surveys, as do selection criteria and analysis methods. The result is a complex mass of information from which to draw conclusions.

Gartner is a leading technology research firm and prominent publisher of cybercrime analyses. Gartner employs professional survey companies to conduct technical research into hot topics affecting the global community. As part of Gartner's analysis process, survey companies ensure accurate and credible results by filtering out refusal rates and self-selection and by calculating tolerable margins of error.

Financial fraud doesn't occur in a vacuum. Malware often accompanies fraud. A recent example involved the sale of fake antivirus software. But the product was only bait; the hook was bogus support from a live agent. Symantec found 43 million rogue antivirus installation attempts between June 2008 and July 2009, and it found an overall malware growth rate of 71% in 2009 over 2008.

Fraud against financial institutions often implies accessory crimes or other criminal activity. A system intrusion may lead to account takeovers, which results in stolen funds. Smishing for identity theft often leads to credit fraud, and phishing is the primary source for advance-fee fraud. One crime often begets another, forming a chain of criminal events, one after the other.

Advance-Fee Fraud

An advance-fee fraud is a type of scam in which a cybercriminal persuades a potential victim to help transfer a substantial amount of money to an account. The victim is offered a commission for facilitating the transaction or multiple transactions. The Nigerian scam, also called the 419 scam, is a prime example of advance-fee fraud.

The Iceberg of Unreported Losses

Beneath the surface of known cybercrime statistics hides a larger body of unknown data. Unreported losses are a major unknown quantity in assessing financial damages, and they are the reason such statistics are only "so-so." Financial services and retail industries don't reveal the costs of fraud openly or freely, so those numbers come mostly from consumer surveys. Schools and colleges also refrain from reporting certain crimes due to social stigmas or concerns about their reputations.

Organizations conceal the dangers of doing business online, such as intrusions and theft, because knowledge of such problems drives off good business. Personal and financial data theft lowers customer confidence. It gives the impression of vulnerability, which ruins consumer trust in a company. Fraud victims also hesitate to report cybercrimes for a variety of reasons, such as embarrassment, privacy, and mistrust. Because few companies and consumers report cybercrimes, all but the tip of the iceberg remains unseen.

The Dark Figure of Crime

Criminologists and sociologists have a term for unreported losses and undiscovered crime: the **dark figure of crime**. It's the amount of crime that remains undiscovered and unknown. That gap in knowledge always casts doubt on the reliability of official crime statistics. As bad as reports may seem, the actual reality is likely to be far worse!

Unreported crime is troublesome for statistics because it casts a shadow of doubt. Several organizations conduct independent surveys to capture some of those unreported crimes, but many remain unknown and uncounted. Sometimes law enforcement agencies conduct their own crime surveys. In every case, refusal rates (that is, nonparticipants) are high, but such studies manage to uncover previously unreported crimes.

Loss Reports: 2008-2010

The IC3 claims there is growing public interest in the average monetary loss due to Internet fraud. The IC3 therefore provides loss estimates across the general population by crime and expresses this information in mean and median averages. Mean averages are sensitive to extreme high and low losses. Median averages represent the midpoint and are less susceptible to extremes.

Reported Losses for 2008

In 2008, the IC3 received 275,284 complaints and referred 25% of them to law enforcement for a total of $264.6 million in damages. And that's just for the victims who spoke up. Countless others lost additional unknown sums.

Among the most prominent scams of 2008 by the IC3's estimate was non-delivered merchandise and/or payment, accounting for 32.9% of complaints. Internet auction fraud accounted for 25.5% of referred complaints, followed by credit/debit card fraud at 9.0% and confidence fraud (such as Ponzi schemes) at 7.9%. Table 8-1 lists the top 10 IC3 complaint categories.

Table 8-1: Top 10 Complaints Received by the IC3 in 2008

Complaint Category	Percentage of Total Complaints
Undelivered merchandise	32.9
Auction fraud	25.5
Credit/debit card fraud	9.0
Confidence fraud	7.9
Computer fraud	6.2
Check fraud	5.4
Advance-fee fraud	2.8
Identity theft	2.5
Financial institution fraud	2.2
Threat (of harm)	1.9

Source: *http://www.ic3.gov/media/annualreport/2008_IC3Report.pdf*

Reported complaints involving the highest median losses were check fraud ($3,000), confidence fraud ($2,000), and advance-fee fraud ($1,650).

According to Gartner, 5 million US customers lost money due to phishing in 2008—a 39.8% increase over 2007. Gartner surveyed 3,985 people to learn the costs and trends for fraud. Results for 2008 show a trend toward higher-volume, lower-value attacks, with 56% of victims recovering their losses. By "recovered," Gartner means that banks or financial services covered the fraud costs.

Whether consumers or institutions should bear the costs of fraud remains a controversial matter. Invariably, the customer always ends up covering those costs directly or indirectly.

Reported Losses for 2009

Email scams using "FBI" in the message and/or the names of FBI officials ranked higher in 2009 (16.6%) than any other fraud complaint made to the IC3. Undelivered merchandise ranked second, and advance-fee fraud rose from 2.8% of complaints in 2008 to 9.8% in 2009. We can't be sure if these trends necessarily reflect an increase in those crimes, but we can say more people are reporting them. Table 8-2 lists the top IC3 complaint categories for 2009.

Table 8-2: Top 10 Complaints Received by the IC3 in 2009

Complaint Category	Percentage of Total Complaints
Email scams using "FBI" in the message	16.6
Undelivered merchandise	11.9
Advance-fee fraud	9.8
Identity theft	8.2
Overpayment fraud	7.3
Miscellaneous fraud	6.3
Spam	6.2
Credit card fraud	6.0
Auction fraud	5.7
Computer vandalism	4.5

Source: *http://www.ic3.gov/media/annualreport/2009_IC3Report.pdf*

IC3 complaints for 2009 with monetary losses had a mean of $5,580 and median of $575. Table 8-3 lists IC3 referrals to law enforcement claiming monetary damage in 2009.

The variance between mean and median values comes from sensitivity to extreme highs and lows. A few expensive cases, in the hundreds of thousands, sharply affect the mean but have little effect on the median.

Table 8-3: Referrals Claiming Monetary Damage in 2009

Damage Amount	Percentage of Total
$0.01 to $99	21.7
$100 to $999	36.7
$1,000 to $4,999	28.3
$5,000 to $9,999	5.8
$10,000 to $99,999	6.5
$100,000 and higher	1.0

Source: *http://www.ic3.gov/media/annualreport/2009_IC3Report.pdf*

The highest dollar-amount losses reported to the IC3 by complaint were investment fraud (median $3,200), overpayment fraud (median $2,500), and advance-fee fraud ($1,500).

Reported Losses for 2010

The IC3's millionth complaint was filed in June 2007, seven years after the organization's inception. On November 9, 2010, the IC3 saw its two-millionth complaint alleging online fraud. Complaints doubled in half the time, and the monetary damages to that time totaled $1.7 billion. Many of those complaints involved identity theft and unauthorized credit or bank account use.

Undelivered merchandise scams (14.4%) edged out email scams using "FBI" in the message (13.2%) in 2010. Identify theft rose a bit to 9.8%. The most significant increase in 2010 was computer fraud/vandalism, from 4.5% in 2009 to 9.1% in 2010. Table 8-4 lists the top IC3 complaint categories for 2010.

Table 8-4: Top 10 Complaints Received by the IC3 in 2010

Complaint Category	Percentage of Total Complaints
Undelivered merchandise	14.4
Email scams using "FBI" in the message	13.2
Identity theft	9.8
Computer vandalism	9.1
Miscellaneous fraud	8.6
Advance-fee fraud	7.6
Spam	6.9
Auction fraud	5.9
Credit card fraud	5.3
Overpayment fraud	5.3

Source: *http://www.ic3.gov/media/annualreport/2010_IC3Report.pdf*

As the IC3 statistics show, criminals actively target bank and payment service customers. But 2010 also saw a focus on US taxpayers through fraudulent correspondence supposedly from the Internal Revenue Service (IRS). In addition, focused attacks have targeted senior-level executives and high-profile professionals in spear-phishing and whaling attacks.

Loss Projections

Successful scams inspire endless variations for years, but a successful trick may find limited use. Misspelled domain names are often a benign nuisance, the only "crime" being misdirecting visitors to unwanted sites. But in December 2010, the IC3 saw this trick used by an imposter social networking site. The fake site was a convincing copy of the original, but it redirected users to bogus surveys offering bogus gifts. Victims received nothing, but the scam rewarded criminals with stolen identities.

Online fraudsters are expected to become even more ambitious in the future. Criminals are taking bolder risks to combat the rising tide of technology and training against online fraud. Awareness training is crucial to defeat online fraud, as technology cannot protect against careless or foolish behavior.

Emerging Trends

Fraud trends show signs of moving away from "net" phishing and toward spear phishing. Instead of general attacks against broad audiences, criminals are increasingly targeting specific groups and individuals. We can certainly expect more of the same: As phishing proves less viable, scammers will turn to smishing and vishing and other new variants. Link manipulation, fake trial offers, advance-fee loans, and job scams will continue to thrive.

Mobile threats continue to expand rapidly. Mobile malware rose 46% from 2009 to 2010—from 704 threats to 967. Like computers, popular mobile platforms attract malware. And why shouldn't they? Many mobile phones store as much private data as computers. The connectivity options are astounding: infrared, Bluetooth, and texting provide some of the many possible inroads.

General consumers aren't the only targets. Online merchants are victims, too. A recent scam targeted online sellers through fake receipts generated by a malicious program. In another case, a malicious holiday greeting pretending to be from the White House specifically targeted government workers. The Federal Trade Commission (FTC) issued an alert in February 2011 regarding scammers who pose as friends or family: The "relative scam" targeted helpful grandparents who thought they were sending money to grandchildren for an emergency.

Speculation Abounds

Scam artists are constantly aware of the latest online trends. Successful cons leverage timing and circumstances to strike as opportunities arise. Speculative articles such as McAfee's *Cyber Threats* and the Better Business Bureau's *Top Ten Scams,* published annually, give glimpses into the possible future this portends.

Uniform resource locator (URL) shortening services are popular among social networks, and 2010 was a great year for their abuse. Symantec predicts more complex attacks that involve abuse of URL shortening, perhaps by criminals hijacking legitimate services or creating services that appear legit.

Fraud trends often follow behind malware trends. Emerging malware threats against mobile platforms can lead to attacks to steal information. Twitter is constantly a target for intrusions and scams alike, and privacy mishaps like those involving Facebook can put users at risk of fraud.

Gaping Security Holes Pose Big Risks

People are always the weakest link in any security chain. People make the poor decisions that undermine privacy and undercut security. An undereducated user is the greatest threat to any secure environment. One person's negligence can put an entire company at risk.

In Brazil, a senior bank official was persuaded by three Nigerian scammers to transfer a total of $242 million from the bank, which brought about its collapse. It was a landmark Nigerian scam. A Nigerian commission eventually awarded $17 million to the defunct bank's lawyer, and the scammers forfeited assets worth $121.5 million. But the damage was done: The bank went bankrupt, and the customers went broke.

As people become increasingly connected, they aren't becoming more security conscious. Popular applications with poor coding or weak security practices may enable criminals to overtake systems and accounts. Unrestricted applications on social networks may access private information and enable identity fraud. And "friendly fire" malware—the kind where Grandma posts a raving review about the iPad she doesn't even own—will increase in frequency. Get ready!

Part 2

Business Use Cases: Anatomy
of Various Cyberheists

9

Bank Scams

In simple terms, a bank scam is an attempt by unscrupulous persons or organizations to acquire financial assets from individuals or organizations, including small to medium enterprises (SMEs).

The focus of this chapter is not on fraud committed against the banking industry. Rather, it is on bank fraud committed against SMEs, often through or by their employees. The Federal Deposit Insurance Corporation (FDIC) insures private individuals against fraud and similar occurrences, but it doesn't insure organizations.

Large corporations routinely purchase fraud insurance or cyber liability policies, but smaller organizations often do not. Although it's good protection, many SMEs see the insurance as an unnecessary expense; after all, the majority of SMEs believe cybercriminals target large corporations. However, SMEs are highly vulnerable targets. If a malicious attempt against a small business is successful and of large enough scope, the company might not be able to recover.

A Sampler of Recent Banking Scams

Many of the methods used to commit banking scams against SMEs have already been presented in this book. For example, social engineering techniques include phishing and smishing to acquire individual or corporate login access at an institution. An organization's employees or customers can also be exposed to fraud attempts via email, social networking sites, and Twitter. Criminals sometimes use malicious programs to drain an organization's assets, which can damage or ruin its reputation or business viability. They may target not only SMEs but also federally sponsored enterprises.

Cybercrime Against an Enterprise

On December 17, 2010, the US Department of Justice announced that a computer programmer had been sentenced to three years in prison for attempting to destroy Fannie Mae financial information. The programmer, 36-year-old Rajendrasinh Babubhai Makwana, had introduced a malicious program into Fannie Mae's servers. The script was embedded in another program that ran routinely on these servers. The malicious script was discovered before it was executed. However, had Makwana been successful, he would have destroyed financial, mortgage, and securities information throughout the Fannie Mae computer network.

In this case, the malicious activity was an "inside job." Makwana was a contractor at Fannie Mae's Urbana, Maryland, offices. He worked there as a UNIX engineer from 2006 to October 2008. In that position, he had access to the almost 5,000 computers in the Fannie Mae network. Makwana introduced his malicious program into the Fannie Mae system on the same day he was fired, October 24, 2008.

At the time of his dismissal, he was ordered to surrender all Fannie Mae–related hardware, including a laptop. Five days later, a Fannie Mae senior engineer discovered the script. An examination of Makwana's laptop as well as a review of computer logs and other records indicated that Makwana designed the destructive script to execute on January 31, 2009.

An FDIC and Patriot Act Scam

The FDIC is chartered with maintaining the stability of the US banking system, and the agency regularly issues warnings about the latest banking scams. In this role, the FDIC is cast as the protector of fraud victims. But the FDIC's name can be misused in an attempt to gain information that could then be used to victimize individuals and organizations with which they do business. You saw one example in Chapter 4; let's look at a more recent example that involves the FDIC and the Patriot Act.

On January 12, 2011, the FDIC issued special alert SA-10-2011. In this alert, the FDIC stated that several customers had received fraudulent emails claiming to be from the FDIC. These bogus emails said that the FDIC, "in cooperation with the Department of Homeland Security, federal, state and local governments," had removed its insurance protection against the customer's account due to "suspected violations of the Patriot

Act." The message threatened to terminate insurance for the recipient's account, and "all records of your account history will be sent to the Federal Bureau of Investigation in Washington D.C. for analysis and verification."

The email also attempted a phishing scam. It requested that the customer click a link, supposedly to an FDIC IDVerify system (which doesn't actually exist), to enter confidential information. Upon entering the fraudulent FDIC site, however, malicious software would be downloaded to the customer's computer.

The FDIC special alert described methods to identify this specific email scam, including the content of the subject line and body of the email. The FDIC, like most other responsible organizations with protective or other fiduciary responsibility to its customers, doesn't issue unsolicited emails.

If you receive suspicious email invoking the name of the FDIC, the Patriot Act, or another federal agency and believe it's a scam, you should report it to the FDIC. You can forward the email to alert@ fdic.gov or call the FDIC directly at 877-ASK-FDIC.

Account Information Scams

As mentioned elsewhere in this book, cybercrooks use phishing, smishing, and vishing scams to steal information. These fraudsters are looking for information such as names, dates of birth, bank login credentials, social security numbers, and other identifying data. Cybercrooks can then use the information they obtain to access banking and business accounts for the individual and siphon off assets.

Cybercrooks also use these techniques to target employees or partners of SMEs in order to access organization assets. They might use these methods against an accountant or a bookkeeper, for example. If the responsible individual can be convinced to click a link or open an attachment, the fraudster wins. Keylogger and Trojan software partner up to help the criminal eventually steal bank account information and funds.

The difference between phishing and the other methods just mentioned is the delivery system used. Email phishing scams are common. But due to the ubiquitous use of smartphones and texting, it's also easy to attempt fraud via handheld devices, using voice over Internet Protocol (VoIP) systems. Another form of fraud is called **phreaking***, and it involves directly hacking telecommunications systems.*

Patco Construction Company, Inc. v. People's United Bank d/b/a Ocean Bank

Cases of bank fraud can set a banking customer and its financial institution at odds. As described in Chapter 7, Patco Construction Company sued its bank, People's United Bank d/b/a Ocean Bank, for failure to "protect its customers' funds against theft."

Ocean Bank said that it employed extremely sophisticated "behind-the-scenes" security techniques to monitor its accounts and protect them from online attacks. However, the Patco lawsuit claimed that the bank's security measures were inadequate and allowed an attack that resulted in Patco funds being improperly transferred. The type and pattern of the transactions were atypical for Patco. In addition, funds were transferred to accounts with which Patco had never previously transferred funds. Further, according to the suit, Ocean Bank allowed the fraudsters to draw on a line of credit Patco had with the bank in order to remove an additional $200,000 of funds beyond the original transfers.

Experi-Metal Inc v. Comerica Bank

In a similar case, Michigan-based Experi-Metal Inc. (EMI) filed a lawsuit against its bank, Comerica Bank, in 2009. The problem stemmed from a phishing attack that resulted in wire transfer fraud. EMI accused Comerica of approving wire transfers allegedly authorized by EMI's controller, even though the controller did not have the right to initiate or approve wire transfers for EMI. The company also accused the bank of having inadequate fraud-detection and monitoring tools.

According to EMI, the bank allowed 47 fraudulent wires to be originated in one morning alone; EMI had originated only two wires over the prior two years. In addition, some of the transfers went to "unusual foreign destinations." All of this activity, EMI maintained, should have raised red flags within the bank.

Consequences to Banks and Customers Alike

The FDIC does not insure SMEs against the kind of fraud described here. However, if a bank fails in its duty to properly protect a customer's funds, the customer may sue the bank to recover the lost funds. However, most cases are settled out of court. *Patco v. People's United Bank* is the first case involving fraudulent online corporate funds transfers that has gone to trial. The *Experi-Metal Inc v. Comerica Bank* case is also moving through the court system. (Both cases are still pending decisions as of this writing.)

These cases should motivate banking institutions to conduct internal security reviews to protect their customers and the banks themselves. It's critical for banks of all sizes to verify that they're taking all reasonable measures to prevent fraud that could result in loss of customer funds.

Banking Fraud and Social Networking

Criminals can use social networking venues, such as Facebook and Twitter, the same way they use email and texting to perpetrate crimes against individuals and organizations.

A cybercrook can spoof a Facebook or Twitter account, and then send a Facebook message or Tweet to an SME employee on the weekend. The message might purport to be from a coworker, requesting that person's login information because the "coworker" forgot his or her own and needs it to finish an important project. If the SME employee takes the message at face value and doesn't use another means of verifying the sender's identity, he or she may end up transmitting the login information to a malicious person. That person then has access to whatever accounts, records, and assets the SME employee manages.

If the employee has access to the company's bank accounts, the malicious person can drain large sums of money or other resources, and the soonest the crime will be discovered is the following Monday. The SME employee will be left holding the "smoking gun."

SMEs Vulnerable to Banking Scams

In 2010, a survey conducted by Ponemon Institute and Guardian Analytics revealed some startling facts about how vulnerable SMEs are to banking scams:

- Of more than 500 SMEs surveyed, 55% had experienced a fraud attack within the preceding year.
- Of those attacks, 58% specifically involved online banking fraud.
- Over half of the SMEs surveyed were attacked multiple times.
- Of the SMEs that had experienced attacks, 87% failed to recover their lost funds.
- About 80% of the banks included in the survey failed to detect fraud prior to funds being transferred.

As mentioned earlier in this chapter, SMEs aren't protected from fraud by the FDIC. In addition, many of them aren't covered under private fraud insurance.

In addition to having their employees divulge sensitive data as a result of phishing and other social engineering scams, bank accounts for SMEs are vulnerable to the same sort of attacks as personal bank accounts.

SMEs and Banking Trojans

Malicious persons can take advantage of unpatched computer vulnerabilities. Newly developed malware is designed to go undetected by traditional antivirus solutions. Various malware types can gather sensitive data from SME computers and servers, including banking authentication information. A single swift attack can remove hundreds of thousands of dollars from an SME's bank account in a short time. Because SMEs traditionally don't monitor their bank accounts daily, the theft might go undiscovered for days.

The probability of recovering the stolen funds declines sharply more than 24 hours after the theft.

Banks aren't obligated to reimburse victim SMEs for their losses. However, they do generally work with a company to attempt to reverse any fraudulent asset transfers. However, the window for doing so successfully is only about 24 hours. Corporate accounts are responsible for any Automated Clearing House (ACH) debits after two days. If an SME fails to review its corporate bank accounts daily, it may not discover the fraudulent money transfers in time to avoid liability.

SMEs and Federal Investigations

Banking fraudsters target SMEs for a number of reasons. SMEs are vulnerable to viruses and other malware, and they tend not to oversee their bank accounts very closely.

In addition, the FBI is not obligated to open an investigation of online banking fraud if the loss is less than $500,000. Many SMEs are unlikely to have accounts that contain more than, say, $200,000. So while these amounts may fall below the level that triggers a federal investigation, they probably represent all the funds the organization has. For small businesses, such losses will effectively drive them into bankruptcy.

Large-Scale ACH Fraud

A single SME's loss may not draw the attention of federal authorities, but the combined losses of a large number of SMEs will.

In 2009, the FBI reported a significant increase in ACH fraud, specifically targeting SMEs such as doctor's offices, schools, municipal governments, and other similarly sized organizations. ACH fraud takes advantage of computer vulnerabilities and malware to transfer millions of dollars in bank funds out of numerous SME accounts. The fraudsters parcel those funds out to money mules—people who are duped into thinking that they are managing payroll transfers for international companies. The mules receive money transfers of less than $10,000 per transfer to avoid triggering a suspicious activity report (SAR) from the bank. Once the mule makes the required overseas wire transfer, those funds are gone forever.

Amounts as low as $5,000 can trigger a SAR. However, the mandatory requirement is for amounts of $10,000 or more. Therefore, most ACH fraud transactions are around $9,000.

The ACH scamming mechanism is an example of spear phishing. You learned about spear phishing in Chapter 6 and will learn about ACH scams in depth in Chapter 12.

Payroll Fraud

Sometimes, malicious parties can add themselves or their proxies to the payroll of an SME. When the bank issues biweekly electronic paychecks, the fraudsters are "paid" along with the real employees. Remarkably, individuals can be added to a company's payroll at the SME's bank of record without the required documentation (for example, a canceled check or deposit slip from the employee's bank or a completed payroll authorization form). In this case, the bank, not the SME, has failed to take the proper protective measures.

This type of fraud requires a coordinated effort, including soliciting the services of a large number of money mules. However, the rewards for the thieves are vast, and the money mules are expendable.

Understanding Scamming Mechanisms

Many of the common methods criminals use to commit bank fraud against SMEs have been mentioned in earlier chapters and in this chapter. Phishing and similar scams are among these common methods.

Malware attacks are fairly common occurrences for both individuals and organizations. However, the malware that fraudsters use against SMEs and their banking institutions most often contains keyloggers. To get keyloggers on systems, scammers must induce individuals who have the authority to make online asset transfers (such as banking staff) to click a link in an email. Clicking the link subjects the user to a drive-by download. Such email is crafted to look like a legitimate business message, such as a notice to upgrade or patch the user's computer email client or office suite.

Malicious people may exploit numerous vulnerabilities, including known computer vulnerabilities that haven't been patched. Also, malware that has been developed recently or that is designed to evolve to evade signature-based antivirus and intrusion detection systems has become increasingly common.

Some desktop and server computers in banking firms used by SMEs fail to use antivirus software at all. In addition, SMEs and banks sometimes either don't have firewalls installed or have firewalls that are poorly configured and don't provide adequate defense against attacks. Alas, this makes the work of fraudsters extra easy.

Also, fraudsters take advantage of poor SME oversight of bank accounts. This lax attention allows the crooks to transfer large sums out of bank accounts. Sometimes such thefts go unnoticed for as long as several days, allowing the fraudsters to transfer assets out of the country.

How to Avoid Bank Scams

Often, employees—including managers and administrators—can be weak links in even an otherwise well-defended company's online security. The first step in preventing SME/bank fraud is to thoroughly train all personnel in the methods fraudsters can use against them to make fraudulent monetary transfers. This includes teaching employees about various social engineering scams, such as phishing.

Training Is Key

Adequate training also means notifying employees that there are no safe communications conduits. Some managers might believe that employees are only vulnerable to phishing-type scams via email, and consider texting, Twitter, and social networking sites to be more secure. That's not true—threats are delivered by cellphone and lurk on all kinds of websites. The best defense is being able to recognize them regardless of their source.

If applications such as Twitter and websites such as Facebook aren't required for business purposes, an organization should use business policies and technical means to prevent their use in the workplace.

After an organization trains staff to be aware of how they can be exploited, it should provide regular followup training. This training needs to occur at least annually. While people are usually vigilant immediately after they have been trained, their threat awareness tends to diminish over time. However, the threat of fraudulent thefts continues to grow, and new variations appear every day.

Often, SMEs, including regional banks, don't have the proper IT or security staff to provide such training. In these cases, the company's best option is to hire a third-party security or training vendor. It's also possible to train in-house staff to provide this service. However, the appropriate staff may eventually leave the company. Or they might not have time to keep their training and security skills current, which means they would fail to keep the rest of the staff apprised of the latest threats and appropriate countermeasures or avoidance techniques.

Chapter 19 provides a lot of information on Internet security awareness training: tips for delivering it in-house, and third-party resources that provide current, on-demand, web-based training for a reasonable price.

Technical Defenses Are Important, Too

An organization may need to hire third-party security vendors to assess the organization's level of vulnerability and to suggest and implement improvements. This can include installing and configuring antivirus, firewall, and intrusion detection solutions to optimize the company's defense against scams.

Both SMEs and the banks they use should use such resources to improve their security. SMEs should also investigate and choose to do business only with financial institutions that use the same precautions and that can ensure an ongoing commitment to online security.

Employees are sometimes taken in by social engineering scams. Therefore, an organization should reduce employee computer privileges to the minimum required to perform their job functions. Not everyone in an organization needs to be able to operate with administrator rights on both the local computer and network levels. Also, the organization should remove any public access to the names and contact information for staff members responsible for asset transfers. This way, fraudsters will have more difficulty learning who to target.

Signature-based antivirus solutions have proven less effective against malware used for banking scams than methods of detection that don't depend on previous encounters with given malware. Therefore, an organization should supplement these techniques with **application whitelisting**, allowing only known software to execute within the company's computer system. The organization should also consider using heuristic detection rather than or in addition to a signature-based antivirus solution, and installing the Trusteer Rapport web browser add-in on computers that may access online banking accounts.

Heuristic detection *is a method of malware detection that doesn't depend on knowing the specific signature characteristics of a known type of malware. Heuristic methods look for more generic elements of programs that are indicative of viruses or other malware rather than those types of software that are expected to be found on computers.*

10

Credit Card and Epayment Scams

Online merchant fraud is a multi-billion-dollar business. Any vendor offering physical or digital merchandise for sale online is a target. Numerous stand-alone fraud-detection device and software solutions are available, but none of them are perfect. In any case, many small to medium enterprises (SMEs) believe they can't afford to purchase such protection. As with banking scams, SMEs are especially vulnerable to credit card or epayment fraud—but no online merchant is immune.

As with many other forms of fraud, credit card scams are not only perpetrated by individuals but also by criminal organizations, usually from outside the United States and Canada. If a fraudster successfully purchases merchandise from an online vendor using a stolen credit card, the item often ships overseas before anyone detects the theft.

If ecommerce fraud involved one laptop here and one flat-panel TV there, it wouldn't be much of an issue. But ecommerce fraud has a vast scope. Every organization—from "mom-and-pop" shops to Fortune 500 companies—is at risk.

The World of Credit Card Scams

Most people are aware of credit card scams that affect individual cardholders. We hand our cards over to restaurant waiters who disappear to a secluded register. They could easily copy the number and use it to buy something online. We enter our card number (the first time, at least) when making a purchase at Amazon. A keylogger could covertly installed on our computer could be transmitting the number to a malicious fraudster. We get a call from our bank, saying that there's been "unusual activity" on our credit card account and asking us to verify our card number. Have we been ripped off, or are we being scammed at that moment by the caller?

Cybercriminals use stolen credit cards to purchase items from shopping and music sites. They also use stolen card numbers to commit much larger crimes. The following sections look at some of these bigger scams.

Credit Card Fraud by Botnet

A **botnet** is a network of remotely controlled computers, usually meant for malicious purposes. To create a botnet, a person or an organization covertly installs malicious software on thousands or hundreds of thousands of computers, without the knowledge of the computer owners. The computers may be located in homes, workplaces, retail stores, government facilities—pretty much anyplace that has an Internet connection.

The average-size botnet is around 20,000 computers. However, some experts estimate that at least 25% of all computers in the United States are part of one or more botnets.

Compromised computers that form a botnet are called **zombies**. These computers may be compromised because they don't use antivirus protection or their antivirus applications are not kept up to date. Owners of zombie computers usually don't realize that their computers have been compromised.

The malicious person in charge of a botnet is known as a **botmaster** or **botherder**. You might hear news stories of how a botmaster used the collective power of thousands of computers to launch a distributed denial of service (DDoS) attack against a web server. Such an attack prevents anyone else from accessing the website associated with the server, essentially cutting it off from the world temporarily. Figure 10-1 shows an example of a botnet.

A botnet can also be used to commit credit card fraud. A botmaster leases access to part or all of a botnet to a criminal organization. Those criminals then make a large number of fraudulent purchases from many online vendors over a short period of time. The use of the botnet hides the true location of the fraudsters, which is often in a country known for issuing massive amounts of spam. Botnets create the illusion that they're in the same location as the owner of the stolen credit card number.

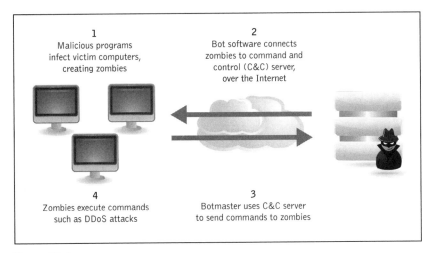

1
Malicious programs
infect victim computers,
creating zombies

2
Bot software connects
zombies to command and
control (C&C) server,
over the Internet

4
Zombies execute commands
such as DDoS attacks

3
Botmaster uses C&C server
to send commands to zombies

Figure 10-1
A typical botnet usually includes thousands or hundreds of thousands of computers.

WARNING!

Thanks to botnets, thousands of fraudulent purchases can take place with hundreds of online vendors simultaneously.

An Example of Botnet Theft

Let's look at the simple example illustrated in Figure 10-2. A fraudster comes into possession of one or more stolen credit card numbers. He or she logs in to a computer in Russia, for example, with an Internet Protocol (IP) address issued by a Russian Internet service provider (ISP). If you could detect the IP address assigned to that computer, you could trace it to a block of addresses associated with the fraudster's true location.

The fraudster accesses a zombie computer in the same area of the United States as the owner of the stolen credit card number. The fraudster then uses the zombie and the stolen credit card number to purchase an item from an online merchant. The item is something that can easily be resold, such as a laptop. The merchant receives payment for the item using the stolen credit card.

The merchant might use a fraud-detection application to verify that the IP address of the customer's computer is in the same general location as the credit card owner. However, because payment is being received through a zombie machine, the general location of the credit card owner and the computer owner appear to match.

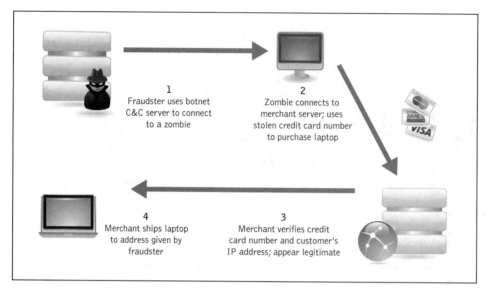

Figure 10-2
A simplified example of using a botnet to commit credit card fraud.

The merchant approves the payment and sends the item to the shipping address the fraudster specified. The item ends up in the hands of the fraudster or an associate and is sold in a foreign market. At some point, the actual credit card owner may notice the purchase of the item on his or her statement and notify the credit card company and the merchant. The credit card owner, the bank, and the merchant are all victims of this fraud.

Because a botnet can be composed of hundreds of thousands of compromised computers, fraudsters can commit fraud on a vast scale. All the while, they appear to online merchants as valid customers using US-based computers. However, they are actually in a different location, using spoofed email addresses and stolen credit card numbers. Merchant losses can escalate into the millions of dollars in a short time.

Instead of using a botnet, a fraudster may use proxy servers to disguise his or her identity. A **proxy server** *is a device that, for the sake of this example, operates on the Internet using an IP address issued by an ISP in the United States. From the merchant's point of view, the proxy server represents the actual location of the customer. But the fraudster uses the proxy as a "mask" to hide his or her true location. The result is the same as if the fraudster had used a botnet.*

Department Store and Private Label Card Fraud

The example of credit card fraud previously cited uses what is called "open loop" cards. These are cards you can use to purchase goods from a variety of merchants. They are the familiar Visa, MasterCard, and American Express cards. Department store credit cards and prepaid gift cards are referred to as "closed loop" cards because you can use them to purchase goods only from the issuing store. Despite the limitations of closed-loop cards, criminals successfully use them to victimize merchants and customers.

Department Store Credit Card Fraud

Bloomberg Businessweek magazine reported an unusual situation involving department store fraud in April 2010. A prison inmate in New Jersey had conspired with seven men in Ohio to use stolen credit card information to rob numerous department stores of up to $1 million of merchandise.

The fraudsters in this case used social engineering techniques to target employees at department store customer service offices. The thieves convinced the employees to release enough customer credit card information to allow the men to fraudulently purchase merchandise from the victim stores. Merchants included Best Buy, Home Depot, Lowe's, Macy's, Nordstrom, and Sears.

The goal of the fraud group was to convince credit card customer service employees to either add a fraudster as an authorized user on the card or to change the authorized user from the actual customer to a fraudster. Individuals known as "runners" would then physically appear at the various department stores and verify that they were authorized users on the specified cards. The fraudsters used the cards for high-end purchases, including big-screen TVs, stoves, snow blowers, and even a John Deere tractor. Many of these items had already been resold before the FBI was able to identify and arrest the fraudsters—including the New Jersey prison inmate who had initiated the scheme.

Gift Card Fraud

Several scenarios can be used to perpetrate gift card fraud. The most common is employee-driven fraud. The most recent survey data available from the University of Florida's Center for Studies in Criminology & Law indicates that store employees are responsible for 62% of all prepaid gift card fraud, with another 13% of such fraud being attributed to lost or stolen cards.

Store employees can use different methods to commit gift card fraud. The method they choose is based on their access to these cards and the card activation process. For example, a fraudster may simply write down the card numbers of gift cards that are for sale and then use the store's website or toll-free number to find out when the cards have been activated. The employee can then quickly use the card number to make purchases.

Sometimes, an employee working as a clerk takes a gift card from a customer who is making a purchase. The clerk then debits the card for the purchase. The card still has a balance on it, so the clerk keeps that card and returns an empty, look-alike card to the customer. The employee then uses the customer's card to make additional purchases until the balance is drained.

Some store employees "clone" gift cards by using gift card numbers. When the card is activated by the customer, funds are loaded onto the cloned card rather than the customer's card.

You'll learn more about gift card scams in Chapter 13.

PayPal Scams

PayPal is a highly reliable method of sending and receiving payments between individuals and organizations that might not otherwise have a common financial exchange method. Millions of people use it. However, PayPal is as subject to fraud as any other financial institution.

Fraudsters attack both individuals' and organizations' PayPal accounts. One common attack method is to use phishing or similar social engineering schemes. This fraud scenario is very much like other phishing scams. A person or an organization receives an official-looking email from PayPal, reporting a problem with the customer's account and asking the customer to reply to the email with his or her PayPal account information.

Phishing involving fraudulent PayPal emails can be a bit tricky. Unlike some other financial institutions, PayPal does send unsolicited emails to its customers. However, PayPal usually addresses the content of the email to the customer specifically, such as "Dear John Doe." Scammers typically address their emails as "Dear PayPal Customer" or something similar. These bogus PayPal emails are sent out to thousands or hundreds of thousands of email accounts, even to recipients who have never used PayPal.

PayPal customers who fall for the scam and give their account credentials to the criminals may find the bank accounts associated with their PayPal accounts drained quickly.

Fraudsters also use their access to "stolen" PayPal accounts to defraud other individuals or organizations. For example, say that an individual advertises an item for sale through an online outlet such as Craigslist. A fraudster sends an email to the seller, expressing interest in buying the item and asks to send payment through PayPal. The seller uses his or her existing PayPal account or creates one, receives the payment from the buyer (but from the compromised account), and ships the item. One of two things will occur at this point:

- The actual PayPal account owner is out the funds for the item.
- The actual PayPal account owner revokes the payment after the seller ships the item, saying the transaction wasn't authorized.

In either case, someone has been victimized.

This sort of scam also works at the organization level if the organization uses PayPal for any of its transactions. Employees who are responsible for authorizing PayPal transfers are just as vulnerable to social engineering scams as other people, and their computers can be infected with keylogger software to collect PayPal credentials. Sometimes, for example, European companies hire contractors in the United States to perform a service. Having no common financial payment method, the European companies use PayPal to transfer monies owed to the contractor. Robbing a private citizen's PayPal account won't yield very much money. However, if a fraudster gains access to numerous corporate PayPal accounts, his or her income could skyrocket.

Understanding Scamming Mechanisms

Although the fraud methods used in the examples presented in this chapter vary, most of them rely on some form of phishing scam, at least in part. Numbers for customer credit cards, gift cards, and PayPal account credentials can all be acquired through some type of social engineering method. The defense against such attacks is proper education for individual consumers and corporate employees.

Highly organized criminal groups typically, but not always, operate elsewhere but victimize online merchants in the United States and Canada. Their success in perpetrating large-scale, very profitable fraud is based on the ability to steal large numbers of credit cards through a variety of means. They also depend on other criminal elements to create malicious programs to form botnets. As you've learned, cybercriminals use botnets successfully to commit wide-scale fraud against numerous online vendors, stealing millions of dollars worth of merchandise, and then fencing or reselling said items in foreign markets.

Although criminal organizations can perpetrate department store credit card and prepaid gift card fraud, the most common scenario for this sort of scam is "the inside job." Store employees are well placed to commit such fraud because they have access to gift card numbers and the card activation process. Also, stores freely allow anyone to find out when a particular card has been activated via their website and a toll-free number, with only the card number that is visible right on the card. Non-employees can also commit similar acts of fraud if they have a method of knowing specific gift card numbers.

PayPal, like any other financial institution, is vulnerable through its customers when fraudsters use social engineering to acquire account access information. While defrauding individuals yields limited rewards, the fact that organizations also use PayPal for payment transfers at an increasing rate allows fraudsters to access larger bank accounts and to acquire more stolen funds. There is some protection provided, although many exceptions to that protection exist, particularly for organizations with addresses outside of the United States.

To find out more about PayPal's rules for sellers, search for **seller protection** on the PayPal website. The Seller Protection web page outlines the specifics and offers a link to more detailed information. Similar information is available to buyers on the PayPal Purchase Protection page.

The Thing about PayPal

PayPal's Buyer Complaint policy is available to assist customers who believe they are victims of fraud, but in PayPal's User Agreement under Miscellaneous Disclaimers, PayPal clearly states that it will not be held responsible for any fraud or deception by any user, whether or not they are a verified user. However, in the same agreement, PayPal states that after a payment has been made, the customer has up to 60 days to click the Refund link on the PayPal site. Even so, the wording in the agreement indicates that PayPal doesn't guarantee that the payment will be reversed.

PayPal's Buyer Complaint and Seller Protection policies are in place to protect both parties in a transaction from fraud, but they apply only to physical, tangible goods and not to items transferred electronically, services, quasi-cash, or any non-physical item.

PayPal's history of reimbursing fraud victims is not entirely clear. However, as reported at *www. steelesettlement.com* in 2008, a class-action lawsuit was filed against PayPal and eBay, Inc., alleging that PayPal's policies and practices constituted deceptive trade practices. The lawsuit also alleged that a breach of the PayPal User Agreement occurred when PayPal customers who had been defrauded were not refunded their money. PayPal and eBay agreed to settle, and the final court approval of the settlement occurred April 30, 2009.

How to Avoid Card and Epayment Scams

Avoiding fraud committed by large-scale criminal organizations using stolen credit cards and botnets or proxy servers can be particularly difficult. A number of enterprise-level antifraud solutions are available, but none of them have been found to be flawless. Also, even highly reliable antifraud solutions, if their technology does not continue to develop to match or surpass high-tech fraud methods, can quickly become ineffective.

Another difficulty related to choosing an antifraud solution is that many such applications offer a single technology that can identify only one type of fraud attack or one element that comprises a fraud attack. This is like a scientist wanting to analyze all the radiation coming from a distant star but using a single telescope to accomplish the task. The telescope can detect only visible light, which makes up a small fraction of the total amount of radiation emitted by a star. The true solution is to employ a detection method that uses multiple devices together to gather the total amount of information the star generates.

Any effective antifraud application must either aggregate the solutions provided by multiple antifraud vendors or must offer, within a single platform, a suite of multiple technologies in order to provide a comprehensive service.Vendors such as Kount.com, iovation.com, and ThreatMetrix.com provide these types of antifraud solutions.

Besides the effectiveness of the antifraud platform, cost is a deciding factor when measured against losses and potential losses to fraud.This is a significant consideration for smaller online vendors who might not have the budget to implement antifraud tools.

Because the majority of department store credit card and gift card fraud is associated with acquiring card numbers and is related to either employees being duped by fraudsters or employees committing the fraud, there are two solutions to consider:

- It's critical to train store employees in social engineering scams so they don't reveal even partial customer account information and do not add unauthorized persons to a customer's account.

- Guarding gift card numbers is especially important. Some stores have taken steps to sell gift cards in sealed containers so that only the customers can access the number after the purchase.This also thwarts casual thieves who "shop" for gift card numbers displayed in publicly available racks.

PayPal takes steps to inform customers of how to avoid fraud by offering advice on its website, but the advice is the same advice you've read elsewhere in this book regarding phishing, vishing, and other social engineering scams. Also, frequent monitoring of banking and payment accounts can allow companies to quickly realize when fraud has taken place, allowing them to stop or revoke payments and to notify law enforcement agencies.

11

Mortgage Rescue Scams

"A man's house is his castle." This famous quote came from Boston attorney James Otis as he argued against "writs of assistance," or warrants to invade and search all buildings suspected in smuggling, including a person's home. Otis's argument was that a man's home is a secure and private dwelling, different from any other building. That was over 250 years ago, but it still reflects how we feel today: We need to feel secure about our homes. That's why a mortgage rescue scam can inflict the most painful and cruel outcome of all scams.

In this chapter, you'll find out what types of mortgage rescue scams exist, understand why these scams are more popular today than ever before, and learn how you can avoid becoming a victim. While mortgage rescue scams affecting homeowners are more prevalent than those aimed at organizations, a business mortgage holder can get duped as well. Predators out there are trying to scam organizations in almost the same way they're scamming private homeowners.

A Sampler of Recent Scams

A sense of security quickly fades when a business owner's cash flow recedes or a homeowner is under extreme financial pressure. Those owners may be tempted to accept help to "rescue" their mortgages.

The mortgage rescue scam is fairly simple and has only a few variants. In all cases, distressed owners reach a similar outcome: They face steep financial losses and maybe even losing their property. This section examines common mortgage rescue scams so you know what to watch out for.

The Phantom Help Scam

In the phantom help scam, the scammer gains your confidence and an upfront payment, promising to act with the lenders on your behalf to rescue your mortgage. The phantom scam is so named because you believe the rescuer is helping you, but the scammer is simply lying in the shadows, doing nothing.

This scam works best when foreclosure is imminent—when you're at the point of "too little, too late." With little time left and no action on the part of the scammer, the foreclosure carries on. The scammer gets a great payment for almost no effort except a sales pitch.

The Bailout Scam

Like the phantom scammer, the bailout scammer exerts little effort, but for a much larger gain: your house. In the bailout scam, the scammer promises to bail you out of your obligation to the lender. The scammer's main promise is to stop the foreclosure immediately. You sign a document that allows the company to act on your behalf with the lender. Other promises might include helping you recover your credit score and get back into good standing with your lender.

For example, after a review of your situation, the scammer may offer to take temporary ownership, with an arrangement to retain you as a renter. Naturally, the scammer insinuates that you'll be able to purchase back the house after everything is squared away. In reality, you sign over the house and lose whatever equity you had to the scammers. If you opted to rent, you would find it too expensive because the scammer makes it unaffordable in order to have you evicted.

The Bait-and-Switch Scam

The bait-and-switch scam is similar to the bailout scam, only more sinister. The scammer does help bail you out of your property, with a promise to help you save or recover it after a short period. The pressure is high to sign a tempting agreement for a new loan or new terms.

Instead, you sign over the property title to the scammer, transferring ownership. Although some documents may be forged or fraudulent, the scammer still receives actual ownership.

In many cases, the victim ends up with no asset but keeps all the liability. The scammers say they want to bail you out of your obligation to the bank. All they really do is bail you out of your property. When the scam works and the property title is transferred, the victim is still left owing the mortgage. Ouch.

Ripe Market = Rampant Mayhem

During the few years following the economic recession that started in 2007, millions of people had to make tough choices about which bills to pay, if they could pay any at all. Foreclosure, the procedure in which a lender reclaims property to secure an owner's debt, became increasingly common. With the booming market of desperate homeowners, foreclosure scamming also became increasingly common.

The FBI reported in 2009 that mortgage scams had experienced a 400% increase over five years. This massive increase is due to organizations offering "mortgage modification" or "foreclosure assistance." These organizations use predatory tactics to entice homeowners to sign over their homes—without recourse.

As homeowners get scammed and report the scammers to watchdog organizations such as the Better Business Bureau (BBB), the number of complaints is overwhelming. Some watchdog organizations have since started redirecting complaints to law enforcement agencies. Law enforcement is relatively inexperienced with such crimes and has little legal support because these types of crimes are too new for protective legislation to have passed.

In short, the market has become ripe for mortgage scams, and there's little to no recourse except to exercise strong "buyer beware" awareness.

Understanding Scamming Mechanisms

It's important to be aware of how scammers prey on others and lure people to cooperate. Understanding their tricks and techniques should reduce your chances of becoming another statistic. Remember, "to be forewarned is to be forearmed." This sentiment applies to mortgage scams as well as all other scams.

Mortgage scamming tricks are simple but effective. Scammers rely on misinformation, pressure, and your lack of knowledge. Further, when you're desperate, their job becomes even easier.

A mortgage scam begins with an offer to help. You might receive an email with the subject line "Stop Foreclosure Now!" or "We guarantee to stop your foreclosure." This creates hope and ultimately trust. With trust, your skepticism fades, even when the advice seems completely counterintuitive. The misinformation begins to erode your legitimate options, cutting you off from those who could truly help you. If the scammer is successful and applies pressure at just the right time, you and your property are separated.

Bad Advice

Mortgage rescue scammers use a number of catchphrases to separate you from your property and money. Let's look at them and examine why they're the opposite of what you need to hear.

"Let Us Help You"

Whether you're actually in trouble with your mortgage, would simply like to refinance, or are just interested in what they have to say, you call their number. A warm ear is all they need: someone who owns a house, a business property, or any other equity and is at least semi-interested. The scammer starts with "Let us help you" and invites you to a meeting. You're hooked.

"We Can Help You Start Over"

At the meeting, distressed owners in particular hear exactly what they want to hear: You can start over, wipe the slate clean, forgive and forget, get back to square one—to where you were before your troubles began. Legitimate lenders don't say such things, but the scammers are reeling you in quickly. They're feeding you empty promises. However, when an owner is facing hard financial times, any offer seems worth a listen, even if it's too good to be true.

"Stop Talking to Your Bank"

The rescuer advises the owner to stop communicating with his or her lender and any attorneys. Of course, this is the opposite of good advice. Once the owner refuses to cooperate with the bank, the bank interprets this as unwillingness on the lendee's part to repay the mortgage or negotiate alternate terms. Foreclosure becomes certain, which is exactly what the scamming rescuer wants.

"We Can Buy and Rent It Back to You"

Scam artists offer to rescue the mortgage for the owner and then rent it back to the owner. If an owner chooses this option, the rescuer's next step is to spike the rent so high that the owner will soon be evicted from the property.

"We Will Cover Your Losses"

Instead of renting it to you, the scam artist may offer you an exchange. In return for paying back all your missed payments, which will help recover your credit rating, the scammer takes any potential gains from the foreclosure sale. A fraudster uses this scam only when he or she knows the home sale price will far exceed the current loan amount and delinquent payments.

Casting for Leads

If you're looking for phone numbers for scammers, you don't have to look far. You can find scammer marketing on fliers, billboards, ads posted in the supermarket, and even hand-written notes left in your mailbox.

In the case of delivered mail or direct contact, you may wonder how the scammers find their information. There are companies that gather, assemble, and sell lists of individuals and organizations suffering with their mortgages. To scammers, such a list is a treasure chest full of qualified leads.

Given the economic conditions since 2007, there are plenty of people having difficulty with their mortgages. Still, getting hold of lists of targeted individuals saves scammers tons of time. On top of the money saved in blanket marketing, the revenue earned from realized scams becomes nearly 100% profit, with little overhead.

How to Avoid Mortgage Rescue Scams

The best advice for avoiding mortgage rescue scams is to avoid having to rescue a mortgage. Sadly, this isn't always possible. If an owner faces mortgage payment difficulties, the first and best action is to speak with the lender about options. The options available depend on the lender and the owner's payment history. Some examples include changing the terms of the mortgage, reducing payments temporarily, extending the loan period, and even allowing the owner to contribute a partial payment for an agreed period. Remember, owners aren't the only losers in foreclosure. Lenders are likely to lose money when a property goes into foreclosure, so most lenders prefer to avoid it.

In addition to working with the lender, a homeowner should seek the professional help of a Housing and Urban Development (HUD)–approved counseling agency. When suffering from mortgage payment problems, it's critical to contact a HUD-approved counseling agency before the foreclosure process begins.

To find a HUD-approved agency in your state, visit www.hud.gov/offices/hsg/sfh/hcc/hcs.cfm. *The advice is either free or very low cost. Plus it's always in your best interest.*

Even without financial resources to keep mortgage payments on schedule, owners who demonstrate good intentions for improving the situation may also improve their standing with the lender. Lenders consider all behavior, good or bad, when making decisions about foreclosure.

Knowing the Vulnerabilities That Are Attractive to a Scammer

If your mortgage is troubled, can you avoid mortgage rescue scams? Yes, but not as easily as you can avoid other scams.

Most scams work on a vulnerability based on misplaced trust (such as checking the box to remember your password on a public computer) or something overly enticing (possibly too good to be true). Both of these apply to mortgage rescue scams but with a key addition: emotion.

Your property is probably the largest asset you possess. With a mortgage, be it on your home or organization, you're emotionally involved. With a troubled mortgage, you're often desperate and extra willing to place trust in someone or something glaringly wrong.

Seeking Professional Help

Consumer protection and business attorneys as well as real estate attorneys are the legal representatives best suited for fighting foreclosure. Most distressed owners are strapped for cash, so incurring additional fees might seem counterproductive. However, a hired professional will ensure that the procedures followed protect your best interests.

Even before you hire an attorney, the following section provides invaluable advice to ensure that you avoid mortgage rescue scams and behave most effectively to save your mortgage.

Understanding What to Do and What Not to Do

Let's start with actions distressed owners should take:

- **Don't respond to unsolicited emails or pop-up ads:** Steer clear of unsolicited emails and pop-up ads online that promise to get you back on track. Falling for such tricks is likely to put you in more trouble than you already face.

- **Communicate:** Be cooperative with the lender or counsel representing your lender.

- **Take stock of your situation:** Determine whether you're close to foreclosure or only behind in payments. Receiving a deficiency notice (because you're behind on one or more payments) is far better than receiving a notice of a trustee's sale (the date is set for public auction of your property). If you're experiencing only a delinquency, immediately act to resolve the debt.

- **Acquaint yourself with the laws in your area:** Every state's laws are different regarding rights and time lines.

- **Choose a legitimate attorney or other counselor:** It's important to seek professional and relevant counsel. Ensure that the person or company you want to work with is certified by HUD (*www.hud.gov*) to avoid another scammer. You shouldn't have to pay for legitimate housing counseling.

Now let's look at some don'ts:

- Don't avoid the problem. Procrastination is a sure way to lose.

- Don't rely on oral agreements. Any offer should be in writing, and you and your professional help should review it carefully.

- Don't be pressured into signing anything before you review every document fully and with professional help.

- Don't surrender principal or interest payments to any entity outside your lender, no matter how "direct" the relationship seems.

- Don't agree to rent the property and possibly buy it back later.

- Don't sign a home-sale contract if such a contract doesn't release you from your existing mortgage.

- Don't sign a quit-claim deed unless your attorney tells you to do so.

Wrapping Up

In this chapter, you learned how mortgage rescue scams can negatively impact homeowners and organizations. You got a sense of how current economic conditions, lack of legal recourse, and human emotions all contribute to the surging market for mortgage scammers. You examined how some common mortgage rescue scams work and picked up tips for protecting yourself from scammers. You also learned several actions to take (and not to take) if you find yourself needing help.

In summary, here's what you need to remember:

- Work with and make payments to your lender. Avoid dealing with anyone else.

- If someone advises otherwise or is acting as an "approved/government" entity, run. If something sounds too good to be true, it is, especially when it comes to your mortgage.

- Act objectively. Take action with as rational a frame of mind as possible.

Foreclosure Fraud: Official and Systemized

For a few years, avoiding foreclosure fraud wasn't as easy as simply being aware and taking cautious steps around individual scammers. In some respects, foreclosure fraud was systemized by the complex mortgage securitization chain of servicers and trusts. This fraud was made possible by forged documents, electronic processing where signed documentation is legally required, and systemized verification ("robo-signers"). While certainly a different scenario than scammers operating as rogue companies, the reputable companies systemizing the disenfranchisement of owners may be considered fraudulent as well.

Mortgage-related fraud has garnered much press over recent years, but only recently has it been scrutinized. Still, it has affected those who make all their mortgage payments on time—and even those who don't hold mortgages.

Systemic fraud is now being investigated. We can expect lawsuits from disenfranchised homeowners and organizations to surface for years to come.

12

Automated Clearing House Scams

Automated Clearing House (ACH) is an electronic network that banks and other financial institutions use to conduct transactions. These transactions use information found on business and consumer checks, normally authorized by that organization or consumer. The transfer might be a single or recurring debit to their account. ACH scams are unauthorized debits to drain money out of accounts.

In this chapter, you'll learn why ACH scams exist and how they've become popular both online via ecommerce and offline. You'll find out what makes some organizations easier targets than others and why. Finally, you'll learn steps your organization can take, both technical and nontechnical, to nearly eliminate your risk of losing money to ACH scam artists.

The Most Lucrative Scam Against Organizations

Organizations of all sizes use ACH to conduct financial transactions in the United States. When your organization makes direct deposits for payroll or issues recurring payments such as for a monthly lease or utilities, you're likely using the ACH network.

An ACH transfer, whether it's a deposit or a debit, requires two numbers: the bank's routing number and the customer's account number. These two numbers, found at the bottom of every business and personal check (see Figure 12-1), are used to initiate a transfer from the payer's account to the recipient's account. This transfer occurs electronically, using the ACH network.

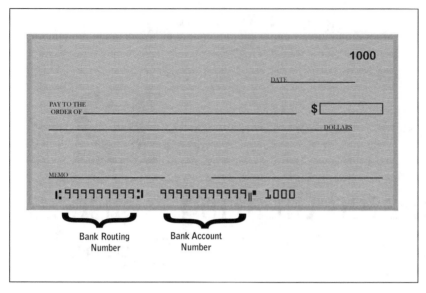

Figure 12-1
Location of bank's routing number and account holder's bank account number on a typical US check.

Sending money electronically is a fantastic evolution in doing business compared to having to visit a teller window for each transaction. However, removing the teller window also removes the bank's ability to verify the customer's identity. Without physical presence at a bank, a customer and someone posing as the customer appear equally qualified to initiate a transfer. This is the main vulnerability that enables ACH scams to flourish.

How Big Is the Score?

The amount an organization or an individual can lose depends on the available balance in the owner's bank account. The more money available, the more the scammer can grab. However, the scammer won't send all funds in one transfer or to one account. Instead, the scammer depletes the account by several, smaller transactions. Transactions for organizations are typically about $9,000, and rarely above $10,000, for reasons explained later in this chapter.

Despite the relatively low transfer amount, this type of crime can be massively profitable. The Internet Crime Complaint Center (IC3) reported that, as of October 2009, ACH scams had resulted in over $100 million in attempted losses. Only a relatively small portion of attempted losses are recovered because the scam works so well. And these are the losses law enforcement has identified; they're likely just the tip of the iceberg.

Targeting Objectives and Requirements

ACH scammers are becoming more discerning than the average phisher and now often target certain types of victims rather than spamming the masses. For ACH scams to be successful as often as possible, a criminal must have the ideal victim in mind. Here we look at characteristics that define the typical victim of an ACH scam.

Small to medium enterprises (SMEs), which include small companies, nonprofits, schools, and other public institutions, are the common targets of ACH scams. Why? Compared to most families, SMEs experience larger, more frequent cash flows. Also, SMEs do not have the heavy-handed finance departments that are common in larger corporate environments. Going further, a corporate firm would have several layers of controls in place in its accounts payable department, making a rogue ACH transfer more readily detectable.

Finally, targeted SMEs are likely to deal with local or community banks and credit unions. The advantage to defrauding accounts in a local community bank is that the ACH transactions are normally handled by third-party service providers.

ACH Scammers Like PayPal, Too

ACH scams are not restricted to checks and interbank transactions. In creating a new account with PayPal, for example, a user must provide his or her credit card number and checking account information. This means entering the routing number and account number found on checks. In short, PayPal is able to use the ACH network for online purchases, making the user vulnerable to ACH scams. Of course, this is not restricted to PayPal, as many online merchants permit ACH debits as a form of payment.

An Example of a Basic ACH Scam

ACH scams follow a known series of steps. An example of an ACH scam is shown in Figure 12-2, but the actual steps are more complex. Having an understanding of these steps empowers you to be more aware and more adept at protecting yourself and your organization. With each step described in the following sections, consider your own organization's vulnerabilities and strengths as a potential target.

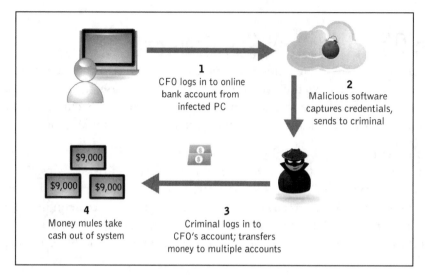

Figure 12-2
An ACH scam in action.

Scouting for the Right Spot

Criminals, no matter how well funded, like to go after easy prey. Anyone who has hunted or fished knows that having the right equipment serves no value if you're in the wrong field or stream. Earlier in the chapter, we profiled types of ACH scamming prey—small businesses, nonprofits, schools, and other public institutions. But even among these common targets, a scammer looks for particular characteristics.

An organization that appeals to ACH scammers advertises the contact person of interest—that is, the person handling funds for the company. Criminals most appreciate an organization that publishes the organization chart on their website. One look on a public website can yield the chief financial officer (CFO) or other person who handles financial disbursements. If the person's e-mail address is also given, that saves yet another step.

Casting the Lure

The next step in an ACH scam is to get the contact person to click to open and install some malware on his or her computer. One example, ironically, is to press a button or link to get better computer security. In most workplaces, the operating system used is some Windows variant. Therefore, a well-drafted email alerting the CFO of a critical Microsoft patch may get the required mouse click, especially if the message is spoofed, appearing as if it's from the CFO's own internal IT department.

Baiting and Switching

If the CFO clicks as instructed, he or she will visit a rogue website that may appear to be the site of Microsoft, a local bank, a social network site, or some other "trusted" site. The malware posing as a security patch, a bank statement, or something personal is now installed. The computer is now running a Trojan program that includes a keystroke logger, waiting for the next time the CFO logs in to the bank's website. During the next login, the malicious software captures the CFO's credentials and passes them on to the criminal in the background. The CFO leaves the website and carries on with business, none the wiser.

Jumping Ship

The criminal now has the user name, password, and any other captured credentials the CFO used to access the bank account. The criminal can immediately log in and initiate a transfer directly. Money is transferred out of the account and distributed to several other accounts, seemingly at the command of the organization's CFO.

And Like That—Poof!—The Money Is Gone

At this point in the ACH scam, the criminal has used the newly gathered credentials to distribute ACH transfers to several accounts. These accounts are likely newly created just for the sake of receiving these funds. There's no reason to believe the accounts are geographically near the victim, or each other, or even in the same country.

Each transfer is likely right around $9,000. This is because any US bank that transfers amounts over $10,000 is legally required to submit a currency transaction report (CTR) due to anti-money laundering legislation passed in 1986. Today, banks have systems in place that automatically send a required CTR, so a fraudulent ACH transfer stays below that threshold to avoid the alert. To transfer over $10,000, all the criminal must do is distribute the total balance via multiple transfers to multiple accounts. And of course scammers do this—until the victim's account is completely drained.

"Mules" Willing, Waiting, and Able

Who collects the money in an ACH scam? The collectors are people who were recruited to quickly receive and turn around the funds to the criminal organization, often unaware of their actual role.

To law enforcement, these people are known as **money mules**. Whether unwitting or willing, these mules immediately withdraw the distributed funds as cash. The mule then wires the cash to places like a Western Union or MoneyGram office, usually in Eastern Europe, where it's finally collected by the criminal organization.

Money mules serve as an interrupt to the electronic process. This interrupt stops law enforcement from possibly knowing which Western Union office the money was routed to without finding and personally interviewing each mule. By the time the law catches up with a mule, the money is long gone.

Money mules are recruited in several ways, but most popularly through online "work from home" ads or through responses to their resumes on employment sites. Mules receive instructions through a manual written by the criminal organization. These instructions provide a full background ruse, keeping the mule unaware of the actual scam. As payment for their services, mules keep a nominal amount or percentage, as instructed.

Trojan Not Required

Using the ACH network for unauthorized transfers can be far easier than the process just described. Instead of targeting a specific person, planting Trojan software, and using captured credentials, a criminal can simply abuse a legitimate relationship between organizations.

Let's say an organization provides account information—that is, business account and routing numbers—by way of a check payment. The payment was intended to be a one-time charge, but the check's recipient still has the opportunity to continually make charges against the account. Obviously, once discovered, these unauthorized transfers could severely damage the relationship. But for some, it may be worth damaging relationships in this way.

The Consumer Angle: ACH Scams Using iTunes and PayPal

Reports to the FBI show that ACH scams are growing in frequency and scale. As the growing popularity of online business and payment methods grows, so does the potential for scamming consumers and organizations.

Take the case where customers of iTunes, Apple's popular online music and media store, saw their bank accounts depleted due to unauthorized iTunes purchases. Each victim had a direct connection between his or her iTunes account and bank account, via PayPal. Users cried foul to Apple, blaming a security breach in the company's iTunes store. In opposition, Apple noted that each user fell victim to emails that led to scammers compromising their accounts. In the end, the connection between iTunes and PayPal accounts on the users' computers was the vulnerability that allowed unchecked ACH debits to the point of completely draining personal bank accounts.

Occasional Scam Elaborations and Distractions

Earlier in the chapter, we looked at how a typical ACH scam works. But some scam artists might take extra steps. Taking extra steps can boost the scammer's chances of avoiding detection or thwarting a victim's attempts to recover the funds—even if it also means drawing large amounts of attention to the scam itself.

Consider an example that involved an ACH third-party provider. Remember that small, local banks often rely on ACH third-party providers for handling ACH transactions. (Large banks normally handle these transactions internally.) In this case, a criminal had taken the extra step of compromising computers of the ACH third-party provider. The scammer then launched a distributed denial of service attack on the provider immediately after funds were transferred to mules' accounts or pickup points.

The DDoS attack was to prevent communications while funds were waiting for mules to collect them, lest the provider and bank try to recall the fraudulent transfers before cash was withdrawn. No doubt the attack brought on a lot of undue attention, but it did reduce any ability to possibly recover funds already stolen.

Distributed Denial of Service (DDoS) Attack

A distributed denial of service (DDoS) attack is an extension of a DoS attack (refer to Chapter 1). However, while a DoS attack uses a single system to attack another, a DDoS attack employs several systems. Using many systems for a DDoS attack can ensure that communications are completely denied rather than disrupted to a lesser extent. An example of a DDoS attack might be hackers conspiring and using the collective strength of their many computers to attack a banking or ecommerce site.

How Fraud Detection Plays into ACH Scams

First and foremost, detection and loss recovery hinge on timing. We discussed earlier that very soon after a fraudulent transfer is made, the funds are redistributed to various accounts, and mules are standing by to make the withdrawals. In some cases, accomplices are even waiting in line to receive cash while the phone is ringing to alert the cash desk of the fraud. But no one wishes for such "luck," nor can they rely on it. Once cash exchanges hands, recovery becomes nearly impossible.

Detection and timing are key to reversing a fraudulent debit prior to cash ending up in the criminal's hands. In this case, detection means watching account activity constantly. Simply noticing suspicious transactions may be too little, too late. By the time a debit transpires, the criminal has already gathered the credentials, tested them for validity by logging in elsewhere, and performed some reconnaissance on the account.

Thankfully, today's technology permits monitoring not just transactions but also the behavior of viewing activity. For example, a bank may employ technology to monitor how often or how extensive a customer views their account. This establishes a baseline of the customer's behavior. Compared against an established behavioral baseline, a criminal's reconnaissance may trigger flags as "out of the norm." A simple email alert or text message can provide enough additional time to investigate further.

Avoiding ACH Scams

Some of the best ways of defeating ACH scams involve having smart practices in place involving key people. In this section, we discuss a few tips that could benefit every organization.

Increasing User Awareness

When dealing with threats of any kind, ensuring that the people involved are aware of the threats diminishes the risk of being exploited. In short, people kept in the dark bump along blindly, while informed people can make informed decisions. This goes for all scams, including ACH scams.

Some may say that user awareness training educates the trainees with "how to" training. However, this is a myth—as long as the organization isn't providing step-by-step examples of how to commit ACH fraud.

As part of awareness training, a user should get an overview of ACH scams, what conditions would invite such scams, examples of signs to watch out for, and, most importantly, what specific steps to take when suspecting an ACH fraud.

Implementing Auditing and Controls

Work environments typically have a single person in charge of some area or set of tasks. Keeping one person accountable for an area fosters productivity. However, it's important to implement independent auditing and controls to prevent abuse within such areas. This is especially true when dealing with ACH fraud that could potentially be controlled by a single person within an organization.

Whether an internal group or external entity performs the auditing, it is essential that the auditing be done independently from the department under review to ensure no conflict of interest or cover-up. In addition, having controls in place, whether technical or procedural, can provide checkpoints that also minimize the risk of abuse.

Reviewing Corporate Accounts Daily

Best practice says we should review corporate accounts daily. Before delving into why, let's first consider how often we review our own personal accounts. How often do you reconcile your personal bank account? How often do you look through and resolve all the transactions? If you do it at all, you probably do it monthly, when you receive your statements. What happens when you discover a transfer you and your family members didn't initiate?

Say that you discover a very large withdrawal or a recurring debit that you're sure wasn't approved. Do you still have a chance to resolve this with your bank? Yes. In fact, even if you skip a month of reviewing your statements, you're probably safe. That's because banks offer a 60-day window in which personal account holders are not held responsible for fraudulent transactions. For up to 60 days, you can report fraud to your bank and you're entitled to full recovery of funds.

Does a corporate account also have a 60-day window to report fraudulent activity? Can it resolve a rogue debit with its bank if the debit is 59 days old? No. How about 14 days or even 3 days? No. Corporate accounts are responsible for ACH debits after 2 days. Furthermore, corporate accounts aren't insured against cyberfraud, as personal accounts are. An organization must therefore review its corporate accounts daily. Put it into practice, make it a habit, and save yourself the responsibility if or when a fraudulent debit occurs. Visit *www.yourmoneyisnotsafeinthebank.com* for more information.

Technology Steps That Can Help Avoid ACH Scams

An organization can take some steps to better defend against fraudulent ACH transfers and to detect them when they occur. The previous section covers critical nontechnical means of combating ACH scams, such as user awareness training and daily review of corporate accounts. Those precautions, however, should be accompanied by technical steps as well.

Implementing Defenses

Using multiple layers of security is important. Much the same way a secure home employs a fence, door locks, and an alarm, an organization needs to employ layers of security for its banking. It should be obvious that access to bank accounts, whether direct or to privileged computers dealing with accounting, must use multiple layers of security.

The Limitations of Antivirus Software

Don't feel comfortable knowing that all computers in your organization have their antivirus software up to date. Antivirus software provides nearly no protection against ACH scams.

Remember that these scams involve malware being sent to an internal computer, either by email or through a visited website. Experiences shared from law enforcement agencies and IT security companies reveal that antivirus software is declining in effectiveness against this distributed malware. Most antivirus companies use known variants to produce "signatures" for their software—hence the need to continually keep the software up to date as the list of variants grows. Unfortunately for us, the variants of malware distributed for ACH scams change far too rapidly for antivirus companies to stay on top of them all. The potential losses to these scams are so great that they justify customization.

Diversifying Defenses

When all the layers of security are confined to one system, the security lacks the depth and complexity necessary to mitigate theft. Say that a legitimate user must enter a user name and password as one step, answer a challenge question as the second step, and then enter a personal identification number (PIN) as the final step—all on the same computer, at the same screen. How secure are those multiple layers of security when the user's keystrokes are being logged surreptitiously? How easy is it for a thief to record and steal all three steps of these credentials? What happens then?

Now, consider a scenario where the user must enter a user name and password combination and then wait for a unique PIN to be sent via SMS. After entering that PIN, the user has access. The system has in fact only two steps of credentials, but it employs a different means—the user's telephone—to deliver the second credential. A thief would have to compromise both the computer and the user's telephone to gain access, after having already stolen the user name and password. Consider how much more secure this method is—and it uses only two forms of authentication rather than three!

It's helpful to analyze your organization's practices through the eyes of a thief by asking "what if...?" frequently. For example, ask yourself, "What if this password were compromised? Would someone need anything else in order to empty the account?" or "Are any safeguards in place in case our supplier double-charges us?"

Bear in mind that users may not welcome adding technical steps for the sake of security. Some users may even seek to circumvent complex procedures if they don't understand why those procedures are necessary. But experience shows that users who appreciate the reasoning behind the technical steps are far more understanding of the added effort and will be less likely to circumvent it.

Minimizing the Number of Accounts and Personnel That Permit ACH Transfers

Earlier in the chapter, we discussed the importance of reviewing account transactions, especially in business accounts where the organization has only two days to alert the bank to problems. Reviewing business accounts daily can be a daunting task, depending on the number of transactions and accounts.

A good technique for minimizing threats—and one that also makes reviewing easier—is to limit the number of accounts that permit ACH transactions. Similarly, limit the number of staff who are permitted to initiate and authorize ACH transfers.

If an account is capable of allowing an ACH transfer, that account must be reviewed daily. If an account is set up to not permit ACH transfers, however, daily reviews are probably not necessary.

13

Retailer Scams

Online retail is hot. Consumers and organizations are increasingly turning to their computers and the Internet to buy products and services. In 2010, roughly 130 million US consumers spent about $235 billion on purchases over the Internet. US organizations spent over $3.3 trillion through the same channels. That enormous amount of money provides plenty of motivation for retail scammers.

Unfortunately, from worthless gift cards to bogus promotions, the retail industry is hit with fraud at every turn. This chapter looks at several different kinds of retail-related scams, many of which are aimed at organizations. You'll find out why organizations make good targets and how potential victims are fighting back. You'll also pick up tips to protect you and your employees from falling for such scams.

Bigger Organizations Attract Criminal Attention

Sophisticated cyberthieves are targeting organizations more and more these days, mainly because the payoffs are big. Business accounts usually have higher credit limits than consumer accounts, and organizations generally make bigger purchases. It's often easier for fraudulent charges—even relatively large fraudulent charges—to sneak by personnel in a busy purchasing department than to slip past an individual who's watching every penny.

Payment management company CyberSource, a wholly owned subsidiary of Visa, Inc., surveys US and Canadian online merchants each year about fraud losses. Cyber-Source data indicate that losses peaked in 2008, at $4 billion, representing about 1.4% of online revenues. These numbers indicate that merchants are managing fraud more successfully. However, estimates of online revenue loss due to fraud were still high in 2010—about $2.7 billion.

The Innovative Cybercriminal

Attendees at the 2009 Internet Retailer Conference in Boston took part in an informal survey regarding online fraud. When asked who's winning the war on fraud, one respondee wrote: "Nobody wins—the best we can hope for is a draw." It was an insightful response. Cybercriminals constantly find new ways to improve old scams and use new technology to create even better and more successful scams.

A Sampler of Recent Scams

Let's look at some of the retail scams that are proving lucrative for thieves. These are the types of scams you and your employees are likely to encounter, including gift card scams, promotion/discount scams, and bogus account credit scams.

Gift Card Scams

Gift cards are a multi-billion-dollar industry in the United States, reaching about $91 billion in 2010, according to research firm TowerGroup. So it's not surprising that gift card scams are alive and well.

There are two main types of gift card scams: those that target cards you buy at a brick-and-mortar store, and those that arrive by email or the Web.

Brick-and-Mortar Store Scams

In a store, retailers most often display gift cards on a rack. A crook can easily jot down card numbers and the toll-free numbers found on the back of cards, or scan the magnetic strip on the card with a portable scanner. Then all it takes is dialing the toll-free number every day or two, entering each card number, and checking the balance. Once a customer buys a card and loads it with money, and the sales clerk or customer activates the card, the crook can quickly use the card to shop online, draining the balance in minutes.

Fancy gift card packaging doesn't always thwart a crook. Depending on how a card is packaged, a scammer can carefully pry the gift card out and then put it back after stealing the concealed numbers.

Retailers must also keep a close eye on sales clerks. A deceptive clerk might keep a stash of used, inactive cards at the register. When a customer buys a card, the clerk takes the payment, activates the new card, and hands a worthless card back to the customer. Or, when a customer attempts to use a gift card, the clerk may pretend the card has no balance and offer to throw it away. After the customer leaves, the clerk slips the card into his or her pocket and shops online later.

The Social Engineering Side of Gift Card Scams

With a rogue clerk at the checkout stand, the odds are stacked against the customer. If a customer has made other purchases on a gift card and is subsequently told that the card has a zero balance, the customer may assume that the card balance had already been exhausted. Some customers are embarrassed when told their card holds no balance and don't dispute the matter with the store or file a claim of fraud. Because customers tend to think of gift cards as "free money," they don't always take the same safeguards or file fraud or criminal complaints as they would if they were using credit cards.

Web-Based Scams

Some clever cyberthieves are taking advantage of gift card exchange websites such as PlasticJungle.com and GiftCardRescue.com. These sites are popular because of the large number of gift cards that sit in sock drawers, unused, every year. PlasticJungle claims there's an estimated "$30 billion in unredeemed gift cards trapped in the economy." Customers can sell or exchange gift cards for a little less than the value of the card. Seeing an opportunity, scammers have used stolen credit cards to buy a bunch of prepaid gift cards and then flip them on the card exchange sites.

Although gift card exchange scams are pretty run-of-the-mill as far as theft goes, some Internet scams are much more bold and sophisticated. In 2010, scammers set up fraudulent Facebook pages with phony gift card giveaway offers. These pages used logos from well-known companies such as Best Buy, IKEA, Walmart, and Whole Foods to entice victims to become fans in order to win cards. However, the registration links on the pages usually directed users to affiliate marketing sites that collected personal data for marketing purposes. The scammers in a Whole Foods gift card promotion attempted to collect sensitive information for identity theft purposes.

With more than 500 million users worldwide, and because of its social networking focus, scams on Facebook can be highly successful—quickly. The IKEA scam lured more than 70,000 Facebook users before the pages were removed. In that case, the scammers created urgency—quite successfully—by stating "only available for one day."

Chapter 14 covers scams involving Facebook and other social networking sites in detail.

Another way to draw victims to rogue web pages or sites is to use **typosquatting**. Scammers set up a fraudulent site, using a domain name that's just a character or two different from a legitimate social or company site. When a person mistypes the web address (domain name), he or she is directed to the fraudulent site, which looks very much like the intended site. The user is asked to complete a survey that gathers the person's name, address, phone number, and other personal information. Upon completion, the person is promised a free gift card. The person, now a victim, either never receives a card or receives a worthless card.

Promotion Scams

Promotion scams come in many different flavors. A scammer may send a phishing email offering something very attractive—for example, free tickets on well-known airlines, free meals at popular chain restaurants, or a free smartphone or tablet PC. Getting this prize just requires clicking the link and registering. But of course, there's no prize—just harvesting of information.

Promotion scams are sometimes targeted to specific people in organizations, such as the president or chief executive officer (CEO). In such cases, the lures include more upscale items, such as flights on private jets or complete vacation packages. The scams generally have the usual result—the victim either willingly enters sensitive information in a rogue website, or the victim's PC becomes infected with malware that harvests data in the background.

Improve Your Website Ranking!

Another type of promotion scam targets organizations that recently set up websites. Soon after you proudly post your new site, your inbox is flooded with offers for website optimization and search engine listings. Although you may have submitted your web address to some of the top search engines, you don't see your organization coming up in search hits, so the offers seem timely and attractive. The scammers know that search engines and directory submissions have lead times, and they're banking on your lack of knowledge of the process, or your impatience. You may pay the scammers to have your organization's URL listed in 50, 100, or more sites, but you get nothing.

Discount Scams

Discount scams work much like promotion scams: They offer products or services—in this case, at a discount—but usually don't deliver. One of the most prolific discount scams involves office supplies, bilking millions of dollars from organizations every year. In the pre-Internet days, scammers routinely called small organizations and purchasing departments, selling bogus copier and printer toner, paper, and maintenance contracts. Now they send emails. Because consumables often wind up in the wastebasket or recycling bin, or hidden away in filing cabinets forever, companies are motivated to reduce those expenses. When an email arrives claiming to save you 85% on printer toner, for example, it's easy to fall for the trap.

Office supply scams have a variety of purposes. Some are phishing emails, designed to gather personal information, usually for marketing purposes. You can spot these fairly easily because you'll often get two or more similar emails within 24 hours of each other (see Figures 13-1 and 13-2). The first part of each email address looks like an office supply company. However, neither domain name comes up in an Internet search, and neither domain name corresponds with a supply company. If you check the domain names shown in Figures 13-1 and 13-2 on *Whois.net*, you see that both domains are registered under the same address, but the company name and contact information are withheld.

Figure 13-1
One email that offers discounted office supplies.

Figure 13-2
A second email offering discounted office supplies.

In other cases, a scammer may accept your order and credit card payment but send nothing in return. Or the scammer might send your first order to you as you expect it. After that, the scammer may send inferior-quality products compared to those in the initial order, or it may increase the price substantially or send and bill you for mystery shipments that you didn't order. Some scammers simply begin sending regular invoices without sending any products, and they use bullying tactics to get you to pay those bogus invoices.

Bogus Account Credit Scams

It's fairly easy for criminals to steal an organization's identity. A person or fraudulent company can usually garner enough information from yellow pages ads or even an organization's website to pull off this kind of heist. At a very basic level, the criminal doesn't need much more than a prepaid cellphone and a box at a storefront postal center to go into "business."

Hiding behind the anonymity of the Internet, such fictitious organizations are able to open credit accounts, buy goods and services, and shut down well before the first credit statement arrives.

According to the CyberSource *2011 Online Fraud Report*, the most effective method of fraud management (in the "validation services" category) used by merchants is the credit history check. The next two methods are contacting customers to validate orders and getting the card verification number (CVN) from the back of a credit card.

Financial websites such as PayPal contribute to the problem. As mentioned in Chapter 10, using PayPal is generally a safe way for consumers and organizations to make online payments, and millions use it regularly. However, almost anyone can open a PayPal account, and it takes little time if you have the required information. It's also difficult for legitimate organizations to know if the company they're dealing with via PayPal is legit.

PayPal requires some personal information, an email address, proof of identity, a telephone number, and bank account information. All of this is easy for a savvy scammer to provide. For example, a scammer can use a fictitious name and address, and set up a free email account on Hotmail, Yahoo, or Gmail. The telephone number can be a prepaid cellphone number or a voice over IP (VoIP) account number, such as a Skype number. Many banks let you set up an account online by simply scanning your ID (which in this case will be fake). The scammer can verify his or her identity by acquiring a fake credit card, a virtual credit card, or a prepaid debit card. It may take some prep work, but the rewards can be great.

The Fake Receipt-Generator Scam

In 2010, scammers began targeting sellers on Amazon with fake receipts. Thieves downloaded a receipt-generator program from the Internet that displays an input form very much like the form from any point-of-sale system. It even includes fields for details such as total before tax. The thief enters phony transaction data, and then the software creates a realistic Amazon receipt and "Printable Order Summary" page.

The thieves then contact Amazon sellers, saying they have a problem with an order, and attach the receipt. A seller might not check his or her records but may simply accept the receipt and send the scammer a partial or full reimbursement.

How to Avoid Retailer Scams

How can organizations defend against devious and sophisticated fraudsters? Education. The more you and your employees know about the individuals and companies wanting to do business with you, as well as the potential scams you could fall for, the better equipped you'll be to recognize and control fraud risk. Cybercriminals are global, and many are well organized and experienced. Learning their game plan helps level the playing field.

Gift Card Scam Protection

Avoid buying gift cards from a store display rack; check with customer service instead to see if they have cards behind the counter. If you do purchase off the rack, carefully examine the packaging to look for signs of tampering. Look for a card that has a scratch-off coating on the back that conceals the card's personal identification number (PIN). If you can see a PIN number, grab a different card.

Watch as the sales clerk scans the gift card and hands it to you. Verify your receipt before leaving the checkout counter, and keep the receipt as proof of purchase.

If you purchase a card online, do so only from the store or company issuing the card. You might get a discount from another source, but why risk it? Don't buy any cards online if your computer and Internet connection are not highly secure.

Comdata, a major processor of gift cards, recommends that retailers run exception reports regularly to uncover "prolific users." These are individuals or companies that make several calls per month or inquire on multiple cards from the same computer. Retailers can block access to those cards until any problems are clarified or resolved.

Promotion and Discount Scam Protection

As you know by now, it's important to think before you click. If a promotion or discount is out of the ordinary, it's probably a scam.

To prevent discount office supply scams, route all purchasing through a designated employee. The employee should issue each supplier a purchase order (PO) with a PO number and manager's signature. This person should also inform the supplier that all shipments must include the PO number on the invoice and packing list, or the shipments will be refused.

If you find yourself in the middle of a scam, don't pay the invoice and don't return any unordered supplies. Contact one of the following for assistance:

- Federal Trade Commission (*https://www.ftccomplaintassistant.gov*)

- Your state attorney general

- Your county or state consumer protection agency

- The Better Business Bureau

Bogus Account Credit Protection

As mentioned previously, running a credit history check is one of the best methods of authenticating a business-to-business (B2B) credit application. An organization should verify and validate all information on an application, including personal guarantors.

It's best to check credit application information against several sources rather than rely on a single resource.

14

Social Networking Scams

As you've learned in previous chapters, phishing takes place in a variety of ways. No matter what methods cybercriminals use, their primary goal is to entice you to click a hyperlink. Once you do, the site you visit may ask you for personal information such as passwords or a social security number. By now, you know not to provide any information in response to a suspicious email.

But even if you don't provide information, just clicking the link and going to the site may quietly download malware onto your computer—a drive-by download in action. Then a keylogger records your keystrokes, and a Trojan program sends them off to the cybercriminals. Malicious hyperlinks can appear anywhere, even on the most popular social media websites.

The most important way to protect yourself online is to follow KnowBe4.com's motto: "Think before you click." If you don't click, you don't open yourself up to potential danger and the many headaches that come with having your money and/or your identity stolen.

This chapter takes a look at scams on social networking sites. While reading the chapter, it's important to understand the difference between the terms *social networking* and *social media*. These terms are sometimes used interchangeably, but they are not the same. One involves relationships, while the other is the tool used to create those relationships.

What Are Social Networking and Social Media?

Networking of any sort involves relationships. **Social networking** involves being actively engaged in online conversations with other people or groups of people. Communication is multidirectional because social networking is all about connecting, collaborating, and sharing information freely.

Social media are the platforms, or channels, used for social networking. Just as radio and television are communication channels, Facebook, Twitter, blogs, and YouTube are communication channels as well. These sites are the tools used to share information, but they themselves are not multidirectional communication. They simply provide the foundation for social networking to take place.

Watch for That Lure; It's Probably Obscured

Many small to medium enterprises (SMEs) spend a lot of time and effort marketing their brands, products, and services on social networking sites like Facebook and Twitter. Today, these social media channels are valuable tools that any SME can use to reach its target audience. The social networking environment feels safe and friendly. Because of this, our guard is down when commenting, Tweeting, or instant messaging on these sites. This is especially true when the communication is associated with a known and trusted organization.

Cybercriminals expect you to be relaxed and at ease on social networking sites. As a matter of fact, they're dependent on your guard being down in order for their scams to work.

However, the enticing ad, the email, or the direct message from a Twitter follower or Facebook friend are all you need to become a victim. The success of every phishing scheme depends on a few things:

- **Your lack of knowledge:** Fortunately for you, you're learning about the dangers lurking on social networking sites. Knowledge of the different types of fraudulent activities in cyberspace is one of your most powerful weapons against cybercriminals.

- **Your lack of attention:** Nobody's perfect. Even those of us who are knowledgeable about the ins and outs of cybercriminal behavior may accidentally click a link. Many times, these mistakes result from not being alert when clicking.

---

*A **follower** is a Twitter user who subscribes to another Twitter user's Tweets. Followers see Tweets from these subscriptions on their own home page.*

Anatomy of a Twitter Phish

The goal of Twitter phishing scams is simply to get you to click. One popular Twitter phish sends you an email notification that you have a direct message. The message may say "Hey, check out my blog post" or "lol, is this you?" and provide a link. The link directs you to a site that imitates the Twitter login page. If you click the link and enter your Twitter user name and password, the cybercriminals have your login information.

With your information, the crooks send out direct messages under your name. These messages could trick your followers into also clicking the link because they believe they have received a message from you. Instead of going to a fake login page, your followers receive spam links that download malware to record every keystroke they make, including passwords and credit card information.

If you're directed to a Twitter login page, check the uniform resource locator (URL) in the address field of your web browser, as shown in Figure 14-1. If it has anything other than the Twitter name, do not sign in. If you do, you could be giving your user name and password to cybercriminals.

Figure 14-1
The real Twitter home page shows twitter.com in the address field of a web browser.

If you click on a link within a Tweet, you also put yourself at risk. Many legitimate Tweeters use shortened links from sites such as *bit.ly* or *tiny.cc* because of Twitter's 140-character limit. Unfortunately, you don't know which links are legit or where they'll take you until you click them.

If you're not sure about a shortened URL, use http://longurl.org/ *to expand the link and see the full URL. Your other option? Don't click on the short link.*

Paying for Services You Don't Want or Need

Cybercriminals are experts at hiding or waxing over information to prevent you from knowing the truth. One example you'll find on Twitter is a service claiming to get you thousands of followers quickly. This is an appealing offer to an SME wanting to build a following quickly.

The criminals say that they do this by identifying other Twitter users who autofollow anyone who follows them. They may also claim to have users segregated by interests or geographic location so you can be sure your Tweets are targeted to the right market.

Even if you're charged for the service and the efforts are successful, cybercriminals who get you followers this way are similar to spammers who sell email addresses. Be careful accepting such offers because you could be accused of sending Twitter spam and be banned from Twitter.

Another example is work-at-home advertisements that promise to help you make easy money. You use your credit card to sign up for a modest fee. Then you're charged a recurring monthly fee to receive additional tips, but the explanation of the amounts you pay is hidden or nonexistent. If you discover any charges, contact your credit card company within 60 days of the charge and put your request in writing in order to get your money back.

Anatomy of a Facebook Phish

As Facebook becomes more and more popular, cybercriminals are finding new and better ways to use it to phish for potential victims. Facebook experienced the fourth largest number of phishing attacks in 2010, right after PayPal, eBay, and HSBC (see Figure 14-2). Phishing attacks on Facebook are similar to attacks through email and other social media.

A common phishing scheme on Facebook involves a cybercriminal using your account to post updates with links on your friends' walls. When friends click such a link, they go to a fake Facebook login page. If they enter their email address and password, the cybercriminal can access their Facebook profiles and the personal information in their profiles.

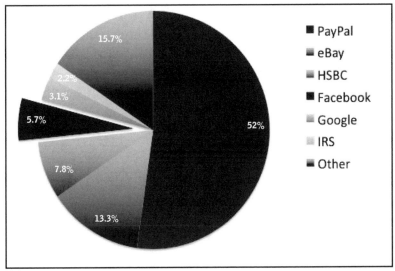

Source: Adapted from *www.kaspersky.com/news?id=207576083*

Figure 14-2
In 2010, Facebook experienced more phishing attacks than Google and the IRS.

In another scam, cybercrooks send fake emails with "Facebook" as the sender. The email says that your password has been reset and provides an attachment that supposedly contains your updated information. The attachment is actually a malware program. When you open the attachment, the malware installs on your PC. The software gathers not only your Facebook password but all other passwords used on your computer.

The following sections describe additional Facebook scams to be aware of.

Quizzes and Other Applications

On Facebook, you'll see quizzes like "What season are you?" or "Which Star Wars character do you resemble most?" Seems innocent enough, right?

Wrong. Every time you accept an application, you're giving a third-party developer access to your profile information. Sometimes these developers are fraudulent marketing companies trying to get you to buy services you don't need.

For example, Facebook experienced a scam advertising an IQ quiz. You click the ad and answer a few questions. Then, to receive your results, you enter your phone number. When you give your number, you are unknowingly agreeing to additional charges on your phone bill each month. Cybercriminals don't display the terms of this fee, so charges can vary from small amounts to costs that can put a severe dent in your budget if not caught quickly.

Instant Messaging

Cybercriminals can get access to your Facebook profile through instant messaging. Once your account is stolen, the criminal can send chat messages to your friends, asking for money. Generally, the message says that you've been robbed and are stranded in another country, with no funds to get home. The message then asks your friend to wire money to you as quickly as possible.

Spamming

Some applications send notifications to all your friends and invite them to use the application because you're using it. The application then spams your friends, displaying unwanted advertising to those who signed up.

Videos on Facebook

You may receive a message with a link that appears to be from a friend, encouraging you to watch a video. Clicking the link takes you to a fake YouTube page where you're prompted to "upgrade your Flash player now." If you download the file, you download and install the Koobface worm. Your computer then automatically logs in and sends similar messages to your friends.

Phishing and Other Social Media

Phishing attackers like to target Facebook, but they're happy to share the love with other social media sites. Just as you should be suspicious of clicking any links on Facebook, you should also be suspicious of clicking any links for these other social media sites.

YouTube

SMEs, as well as large corporations, are turning to YouTube to make money or strengthen their brands through video sharing. The intent is to ultimately drive traffic to their own websites. Traffic-generator companies advertise on YouTube and via email that they will help you "earn subscribers," but they are usually fraudulent companies looking for victims. The thieves ask for your user name and password, and often your credit card number. As is the case with most phishing schemes, you're at risk of identity theft, account theft, or malware infection.

Some scamsters take advantage of current disasters, such as the Japan earthquake and tsunami in March 2011, by posting videos promising miracle stories from survivors. The video is supposedly hosted on a different site because of copyright issues. If you click the link, you may be presented with a survey you're required to complete to view the video. The survey is actually a phishing scam. Or clicking the link results in a pop-up window that states you must install a toolbar or some other software to view the video, but the program is malicious.

In 2010, a staggering 3 million YouTube pages were covered by an invisible Flash object/layer that took the user to a fake antivirus page. From that page, malware could download without the user's knowledge. The site came up when searching "Hot Video."

LinkedIn

Cybercriminals not only steal identities on Facebook and Twitter, but on LinkedIn as well. Most of us believe that LinkedIn is safer because it's more professional, but that's not the case. Cybercriminals create false profiles to get access to a variety of individuals throughout the site. The criminals often join group discussions, and then post comments with fake freelance job offers and links to their (rogue) websites. They also may simply "spam" discussions with marketing-related comments and links.

Blogs

Setting up fake blogs is a popular way to sell everything from office supplies to online training to subscription services. For example, a blog may follow an IT manager through a series of management training courses. The manager writes weekly about the materials and topics covered in the course, and is open about his or her struggles and victories throughout. The manager also includes information about upcoming class dates and cities where training is offered, along with a website where readers can sign up and pay for the training.

While the charges are real, the training isn't. Neither is the IT manager. Scams like this are difficult to detect because you relate to the IT manager through the blog posts. Once you feel you "know" this person, it's much easier to hand over your credit card so you can attend the next class or training session.

Advertisements for these types of blogs tend to appear on social networking communities that are IT-related, so be aware, do your homework, and use good judgment before you buy.

How to Avoid Phishing on Social Media

The following are some general precautions you should take when using social media sites:

- Do not click on links in any email from a social networking site. If you think an email might be legitimate, ask the sender by phone or in person if he or she sent the email. If the link is for a website, go to the site directly by typing the address into your web browser.

- Beware of anyone asking for money through a social networking site. Cybercriminals might be able to get enough information to impersonate a coworker or an acquaintance.

- Do not upload updates from an email link. Always go to the site directly through your web browser.

- Always check the URL before logging into any social networking site.

- Never re-enter your login information after you've already logged into the social networking site.

- Keep your security software up to date and make sure it runs continuously.

- Google your organization occasionally to see what kind of information you find about it on the Internet. Cybercriminals can also find that information and use it to hack your social media and other accounts.

- If your account has been hacked, change your password immediately.

- Make your passwords stronger with special characters and change your passwords often.

- Pay attention when reading emails and when you're on social networking sites. Try not to read when you're tired and not alert enough to spot potential phishing or scam activities.

- Don't share sensitive information on any social networking site.

- If you freely accept every invitation to follow, friend, or connect, be careful about the information you share. Adjust your settings to let people see only what you want them to see.

- Be cautious of any shortened URLs like *bit.ly* or *tiny.cc*. If you receive a link from a colleague and feel it's legitimate, cut and paste the link into *http://longurl.org/* to determine the actual target address.

Twitter Precautions

Be extremely wary of short links that offer you coupons, prizes, gift cards, or work-at-home opportunities.

Many free services, such as Twitpic, are designed to enhance your time spent on Twitter. However, don't assume that every service with "twitt" or "tweet" in its name is legitimate. If you're interested in using a free app or service, search for the name on the Internet and read independent reviews first.

Monitor Twitter's Spam Watch for updates on spam and scams. Just follow *twitter.com/spam* to get started.

Facebook Precautions

SMEs should regularly review the security of their company Facebook pages and any associated campaigns. Adjust your Business Page settings and permissions, and be sure to continuously monitor the comments and discussions taking place on your Business Page wall.

In addition, listing your workplace or company affiliation on Facebook is fine as long as you protect yourself while you're at work. Edit your personal profile application and website settings on Facebook to limit access to your information. Here's how:

1. On the top right of your Profile page, click **Account > Privacy Settings**. The Choose Your Privacy Settings page appears.

2. In the Apps and Websites section at the bottom of the page, click **Edit your settings**. The Choose Your Privacy Settings > Apps, Games and Websites page appears.

3. Edit the appropriate settings to adjust who sees your information.

YouTube Precautions

To protect yourself when using YouTube, turn off Flash, even though doing so can prevent some legitimate sites from displaying properly. Use caution if you turn Flash back on to view videos. In addition, be very cautious in clicking any links that may take you out of the YouTube site.

LinkedIn Precautions

Before accepting an invitation on LinkedIn, check out the person's profile. If it looks suspicious, click Ignore to refuse the invitation to connect. The same principle applies to group discussion links; to avoid a scam, check the profile of any group participant who offers potential work.

Blog Precautions

Here are a few ways to determine whether you're reading a fake blog:

- Do the photographs of the blogger seem too "slick"?
- Does it have fake endorsements by someone like Dr. Oz or Oprah?
- Does the offer for free items seem too good to be true?
- Is there a deadline for purchasing?

If you suspect you're reading a fake blog, don't buy. You could be handing your credit card information to a cybercriminal who is waiting to take advantage of you.

Part 3
Countering Cybercrime

15

Fundamentals of Safe Computing

As we use computers at work and at home, we're responsible for those systems. One of the best ways to fulfill this responsibility is to act as good cybercitizens. This means becoming educated on best practices for safe computing and executing them diligently.

This chapter examines safe computing practices at the user level (on desktops and laptops), on networks, and beyond.

What Does Safe Computing Mean?

Safe computing is the application of safeguards and precautions that protect you from becoming a victim of cybercrime. To ensure that you're safe from cybercrime—or at least safer—you must educate yourself and your employees about the dangers and threats that exist online.

Becoming aware of various options to secure systems—such as using encryption, complex passwords, and physical security—allows you to select and use multiple layers of defense. The more layers of defense you can erect and use, the safer your computing experience will be!

It's just as important to use protection tools and techniques as it is to understand what types of attack may come your way on the Internet.

Fraudulent activity can originate from the Internet or internally on your own networks. You should know how to recognize and respond appropriately to attacks, regardless of their origin. Also, by arming yourself with the proper protective tools, you can mount a more effective response. Ultimately, learning and understanding how to recognize and counter cybercriminal methods and techniques is essential to practicing safe computing.

Best Practices for Safe Computing

You can employ many methods to create a safer computing environment. In this section, we'll discuss some of the most effective best practices. If you apply them correctly and consistently, you can mitigate the risk of successful attacks and criminal action. This list is by no means exhaustive, but it does include options for various situations.

Most of these best practices for safe computing bridge the gap between home and work environments. Certain concepts, such as using strong passwords, apply in both cases. Others may make sense only in one world or the other, such as network protection, which is too expensive to implement on most home networks but typical on organization networks.

Physical Security

A common idiom states, "Possession is nine-tenths of the law." In the case of cybercrime, possession typically allows for abuse of the law. It's often said that if an attacker has unrestricted access to your computer, he owns it and there's nothing he can't do. If thieves take physical possession of property that doesn't belong to them, they have an opportunity to exploit that property for gain.

It's very difficult to protect something that's not in your possession. If a thief steals your laptop, for example, you can't directly protect that laptop. Hopefully you took measures to protect information on the system, such as using a login fingerprint scanner, backing up data regularly, using encryption, and installing a tracking program or chip. Many people don't. A thief will go to work quickly, using a number of software programs to obtain login access to the system. If the laptop contains sensitive financial information, such as bank account or credit card numbers, the criminal hits the jackpot once login is achieved. To reduce the opportunity for physical manipulation and, in turn, theft, you need to take measures to establish physical security.

Physical security comes in many forms. One of the simplest forms is a lock and key. In larger organization environments, IT staff typically keep servers in locked server racks, in locked server rooms. By limiting who has physical access to the machines, you reduce the opportunity for physical theft.

In both cubicles and home offices, a lot can be said for storing laptops in locked cabinets when you're not using them. Also, most laptops ship with built-in locking ports that let you attach laptops to desks or racks. You can purchase aftermarket locking devices to secure workstation and desktop machines, too. By maintaining physical control over hardware, you make it more difficult for criminals to obtain access to data. If they must use the network to get to a computer, protection is more easily implemented because the point of entry is narrower. (You'll learn about network safeguards later in this chapter.)

The Merits of Logging Off

Another method for protecting systems is to enable and enforce account logoff or machine locking once a specific idle period elapses. This ensures that a hapless user doesn't become victim to a criminal because that user left a workstation logged in and unattended.

If an attacker gains physical access to a machine that's still logged in but not in use, the hard work required to access the system is already done. Getting to the good stuff—the data—is usually easy at this point. That's why automatic lockout or logoff is such a good idea and an important part of safe computing practices.

Passwords

The primary authentication mechanism used in computing today is account names with associated passwords. **Authentication** is the process of identity verification, which can take a number of forms. A user name and password combination is a simple form of authentication. These credentials are pieces of information a user must know to be successfully admitted and granted access to resources in an environment.

A user who presents a valid user name and password for authentication validates identity. Using only a user name and password combination for this validation is called **one-factor authentication** or single-factor authentication. This is because only a single form of identification (the user name/password combination) is requested and validated for granting resource access. Using additional verification methods improves security. This is referred to as **multi-factor authentication**, in which two or more security mechanisms are used.

Two-factor authentication typically includes something the user knows, such as a user name and password combination, as well as something the user has, such as a smart card or an access token. Environments where more extreme security measures are required often use multi-factor authentication with three or more security mechanisms. In addition to something the user knows (such as a user name and password) and something the user has (such as a smart card or an access token), you can require biometrics to enforce something the user "is." Fingerprints and retinal patterns are examples of unique physical traits that can be collected with biometric scanners.

And You Are . . .?

Authentication applies to everyday life as well as the computing world. Let's say you call a plumbing company to request service for leaky pipes. When the plumber knocks on your front door, you might notice that he's wearing a uniform representing his employer and maybe driving a company truck or van. If you're still not convinced, you might ask to see his company ID or driver's license. Then you would let him in. Each of these activities serves as identity validation and helps prevent the social engineering practice of impersonation.

Using Secure Passwords

These days, we need passwords for just about everything: logging in to a computer, accessing corporate resources at the office, or banking online and checking personal email at home. With cybercrime on the rise, and because of the growing portfolio of passwords we must constantly manage, it's increasingly important to ensure that people use safe passwords.

The function of passwords in any corporate, personal, or Internet computing environment is to provide security through identity verification. To improve the strength of a password, you must consider its characteristics. Just as "loose lips sink ships," poor passwords can inadvertently grant attackers access to private resources.

The are several characteristics of a strong password:

- Is at least eight characters long
- Contains a combination of numbers, letters, and symbols
- Contains a combination of uppercase and lowercase letters
- Is not a common name or user name
- Is not a word in the dictionary of any language

Passwords hold the key to data access. Whether a password protects a single file or is used in combination with a login name, you're only as safe as the strength of your password.

Use the Microsoft Safety & Security password-checker website to test the strength of a password:
https://www.microsoft.com/security/pc-security/password-checker.aspx?WT.mc_id=Site_Link

The longer a password stays the same, the greater the chances that an attacker will learn the password and steal information. It's considered a best practice to force users to change passwords regularly. The same principle applies to home offices and password-protected websites. Because the latter is usually not enforceable, encourage your employees to take it upon themselves to change their passwords frequently.

Password safety must be taught in order for users to understand appropriate password usage habits. Some key concepts you should communicate to employees include the following:

- Change your passwords frequently—at least every 90 days.
- Choose strong passwords that are difficult to guess.
- Use different passwords for different accounts.
- Use different passwords for public accounts, such as Hotmail or Gmail, and personal accounts with sensitive data, such as banking sites.
- Do not use personal information such as birthdates, addresses (in part or whole), children's names, pets' names, and so on.
- Do not share your passwords with others.
- Do not write down passwords. Instead, use phrase techniques to create a strong password that is easy to remember.
- Do not keep a password file on your computer.
- Never use public computers or public Wi-Fi services to access password-protected websites.
- Never respond to email requests for your password.

Phrase techniques *produce strong passwords. One technique involves creative transformations for a sentence so that, for example, "I never eat rye bread" becomes iN3V3RtaeWRYdearb. Another technique uses creative abbreviations, turning "I have two left feet and crossed eyes" into IH2lf&x0><0. Such passwords are fairly easy to remember yet nearly impossible to guess.*

Social Engineering and Phishing

Social engineering is one of the most problematic attack techniques to combat. It preys on our nature as human beings and is therefore difficult to counter by using technology. User education is most effective at stopping a social engineer. Users who are aware of the potential for social engineering attacks and learn to recognize them can use simple methods to thwart these attacks successfully.

As described in Chapter 1, phishing is a type of social engineering that's executed through unsolicited email messages. Figure 15-1 shows a sample phishing email message.

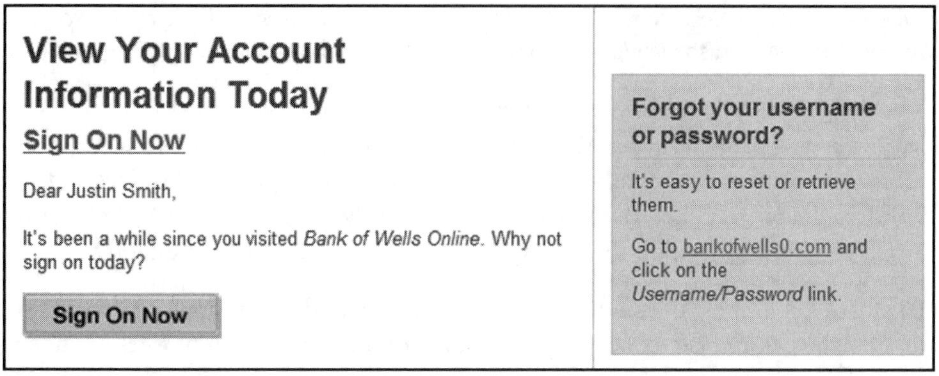

View Your Account Information Today

Sign On Now

Dear Justin Smith,

It's been a while since you visited *Bank of Wells Online*. Why not sign on today?

Sign On Now

Forgot your username or password?

It's easy to reset or retrieve them.

Go to bankofwells0.com and click on the *Username/Password* link.

Figure 15-1
An example of a fictitious phishing email.

Notice that the email message looks as if it came from the user's bank. The formatting most likely matches that of the bank's typical email messages. The name of the bank looks correct, and the user's name even looks properly addressed in the message.

At first glance, this email message looks legitimate. It appears as though the bank sent it to ask the customer to log in to his account. However, notice that the link provided on the right side of the message has an extra 0 in it. If you hovered your mouse pointer over the Sign On Now button, you would discover the same thing. The email message did not originate from the bank. It's actually intended to direct the user to a malicious website. The look and feel of the rogue website would be similar to the look and feel of the actual banking site, but a criminal, not the bank, would receive any data the unwitting user entered.

With the user's name and password, an attacker could go to the real banking site, access the victim's account, and steal money. If the victim uses the same user name and password on many sites, the cybercriminal has also obtained credentials to many of that person's accounts. The results could be catastrophic for the victim. Damage could range from petty monetary theft, to a complete drain of financial resources, to full-blown identity theft.

Should I or Shouldn't I?

Users must be educated to understand that it's typically not safe to divulge sensitive information. For example, they should **never** respond to unsolicited requests for sensitive information. The request ploy may vary, but the response should remain consistent. Don't do it!

If a user initiates contact, a request for sensitive information is usually warranted. For instance, if you call your bank to request a change to your account, the bank first verifies your identity. The bank may do this by asking for the passcode you selected when you established the account. In addition, the bank would ask for other information to authenticate you as a valid account holder, such as your name, account number, and possibly address or phone number.

The same concept holds true for websites that are password protected. Let's say you type the address of your bank or email provider in a web browser and press Enter. You can typically be assured that you're connecting to the authentic site. However, if your PC is infected with malware that redirects your web requests, you may still be at risk. This is one reason that an up-to-date anti-malware program is also a must-have for safe computing.

Look for SSL to Keep You Safe

It's relatively easy to ensure that you're in a secure computing environment. Before entering any sensitive information into a web form, look for an indication of Secure Sockets Layer (SSL). SSL is an encryption technology that, among other things, lets you connect to websites securely. (You'll learn more about encryption later in this chapter.)

Different web browsers display different SSL indicators. Figure 15-2 shows the SSL indicators in Mozilla Firefox and Microsoft Internet Explorer. Typically, a lock icon is displayed somewhere in the browser screen and the website address is prefaced with the letters *https*. The letter *s* in *https* indicates that SSL encryption is in use.

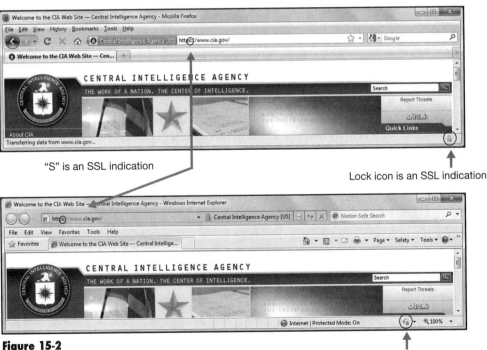

"S" is an SSL indication

Lock icon is an SSL indication

Figure 15-2
SSL indicators in Firefox (top) and Internet Explorer (bottom).

Lock icon is an SSL indication

If a connection is *not* secured with SSL, it transmits data across the Internet as clear text. **Clear text** is unencrypted text that can be read by anyone who captures the transmission.

Never enter any sensitive information at a website before checking the web browser for some definite indication that SSL is in use.

If you have followed best practices and taken safety precautions, you may decide to follow through with an online activity anyway. However, think carefully about what kind of site you're visiting and what kind of information you're being asked to provide. In some circumstances, you should be skeptical and suspicious. If you doubt the legitimacy of any situation, refuse to provide sensitive data to the requesting party. Chances are a cybercriminal is trying to trick you into providing private information.

Network Security

Defense in depth uses multiple layers of security in a network. For instance, instead of allowing users from the Internet to directly access your internal network, you would implement a firewall. **Firewalls** are hardware devices or software that restrict the types of traffic that may flow into, through, and out of an internal network. Firewalls use rules to control traffic flow. You create a specific list of rules that allows only certain types of traffic onto the network, and you block other traffic.

By using components such as proxy servers, you can further extend network control to web-based traffic. A proxy server allows or blocks access to particular websites for users within the network. When a proxy server is deployed, administrators configure workstation web browsers, such as Internet Explorer or Firefox, to send all website requests to the proxy server. As a result, the proxy server acts as a gatekeeper for Internet-bound requests and can selectively allow or deny access to specific Internet destinations.

You should also enforce access controls (of which authentication is a part), and minimize the permissions (level of access) granted to users for system resources. Grant users and administrators the lowest level of access required to perform their job functions and no more. This is referred to as the principle of least privilege; access controls and least privilege are covered in Chapter 17.

Firewalls and proxy servers, along with user access control, are common components of a defense-in-depth strategy.

Encryption

Encryption is the process of making clear text unreadable. Before anyone can read encrypted text, it must first be decrypted. By encrypting sensitive data wherever possible, you greatly reduce opportunities for criminals to steal sensitive information.

An internal network is a common attack point for cybercriminals. Data being transmitted locally from point A to point B is typically sent unencrypted. This allows an attacker who's eavesdropping to capture a copy of the data and read the contents.

Network administrators and attackers alike use a network tool commonly referred to as a **sniffer**, **packet analyzer**, or **protocol analyzer**. This tool captures data transmitted across a cable or wireless connection and lets the user analyze the data to determine its payload. Unlike clear-text data, encrypted data that's captured by a sniffer is difficult or impossible to read.

As you learned earlier, SSL is an encryption technology that greatly contributes to safe computing on the Internet. By securing transmissions from web browsers to web servers, information such as credit card numbers and social security numbers can be transmitted in an illegible format, therefore enhancing protection. Consider encrypting data on the internal network as well for a very high level of security.

Public Use of Private or Public PCs

Public PCs, such as computers in libraries or Internet cafes, present a security risk to users. The security of the PC and its Internet connection are out of your control. An attacker can install malicious software on the PC to capture user names and passwords. A packet sniffer may even be running on the network, capturing your Internet activities. All you have to do is access your bank or a similar website from a compromised public PC, and your credentials are stolen in seconds.

Public use of private PCs is common in airports and coffee shops, and it has similar implications to using public PCs. By connecting your laptop to a public network, such as free Wi-Fi, you're taking on all the risks that come with an unmanaged, open network. Other computers in the network may have viruses that try to spread to your machine. You can also become infected with keystroke loggers and Trojans.

Attackers often set up free Wi-Fi networks in public places to lure unsuspecting victims. Once you connect to the rogue Wi-Fi network, the attacker may intercept your emails, get your user names/passwords, or execute a malicious attack on your computer. You most likely won't notice a thing.

So, if you need to connect to a public Wi-Fi network, ensure that you're clicking a valid and safe network name. At the airport, look around for a sign that advertises the Wi-Fi network. At a coffee shop, ask the barista. Do not attempt to connect to any other available Wi-Fi networks in the area. Make sure your PC's firewall is on, lock down your Public wireless connection settings (see Figure 15-3), and encrypt sensitive files or folders on your hard drive ahead of time, if possible.

If you don't need Internet access but just want to use your PC, shut off your wireless card or adapter. Either pop the card out of the slot, or press the Fn key and the F key associated with your wireless connection.

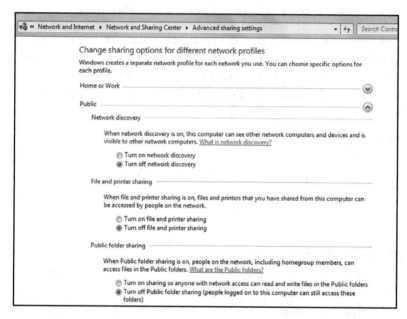

Figure 15-3
Locking down Public wireless connection settings in Windows 7.

Anti-Malware

Recall from Chapter 1 that malware is any software that's installed on a computer with the intention of executing malicious code and/or causing damage. Typically, the software installs without the owner's permission.

Malware comes in many forms, including viruses, worms, Trojans, spyware, and adware. The best protection against malware is to install anti-malware protection software. Antivirus and antispyware software comes in stand-alone packages and as part of full-featured suites. Regardless of which software you select, it's important to take these two key steps:

- Always ensure that the software is up to date.
- Never circumvent security protection mechanisms.

VIPRE Antivirus Business, by GFI, is a highly rated anti-malware package that's ideal for the small to medium enterprise (SME) environment. Visit www.gfi.com for details.

Safe Internet Use

Safe Internet use starts with using safe computing habits while surfing the Internet. **Safe surfing** refers to a user's behavior when browsing the Web. Cybercriminals will try many different ways to get sensitive information or take your money in a scam. You have to watch out for their tactics.

Watch What You Download

First, avoid questionable downloads. Never click on a pop-up or pop-under ad when using a web browser. Although some are completely harmless, most are not. Many people fall for "optimize your PC" or "disinfect your PC" pop-ups. Clicking such ads guarantees a rogueware (spyware or other malware) infection on your PC.

Also, scrutinize any software you intentionally download from the Internet. The enormous amount of free software on the Internet is tempting, but it's best to visit the manufacturer's website directly or a trusted download site, such as CNET's *download. com*. Clicking just any link that comes up in a list of search hits can have devastating effects.

For example, say that your coworker gives you a web camera he no longer uses. You attach it to your PC but don't have the software to run it. You search the Internet, click the first link at the top of the results list, download software, and install it. After a few days, your PC seems sluggish, and the hard drive seems to be working overtime. You run an antivirus scan, which finds a handful of malware programs. If you're able to quarantine the malware without losing data or your passwords, you're lucky. More likely, by the time you detect the malware, your PC has been compromised—along with your bank and credit card accounts.

Don't Click Any Ol' Link

We've said it countless times in this book because it's so important: Never click links in unsolicited emails or on suspect websites. Email from a trusted source is generally safe. However, ensure that the email is actually from the trusted source before taking action. Chapters 1, 3, and 4 dissect some phishing examples to help you avoid scammers and attackers.

Individuals and organizations should use spam filters to reduce the amount of email from untrusted or unsolicited sources. Internet email providers have built-in spam-filtering tools you can configure to meet your needs.

16

Syncing Up Security Policies, User Training, and Monitoring

To some extent, establishing and maintaining proper information security is a balancing act. It involves formulating security policies to state what assets are worth protecting, how far such protection should go, and what kinds of protection should be applied to them. User training helps to address the all-important human element in security. Finally, monitoring is necessary to ensure that security is working and protecting the right things. It also enables organizations to react quickly and decisively when a security breach occurs.

This chapter addresses security policies, user training, and monitoring, aimed at protecting small to medium enterprises (SMEs). Failing to implement even one of these components can greatly increase your organization's risk of attack or security breach.

Security Policies

A **security policy** is a document that establishes how an organization secures its facilities and information technology (IT) environment. Large organizations may have several policies, in separate documents, that represent a collective security policy.

The more complex the policy, the more difficult it is to maintain. In an SME environment, a best practice is to designate one person to be in charge of policy maintenance. That person can assign parts of the policy to different personnel, but he or she should be aware of all policy changes and any ripple effects.

The physical security of all things IT, such as switches, routers, and servers, must be addressed. In addition, the policy should outline protection methods used to safeguard IT assets from unauthorized access and exploitation. It should also address the actions administrators and security personnel will take if a security breach occurs.

Why Security Policies Vary

Every organization is unique, and even departments within the same organization might face different threats. This leads to security policies varying greatly among organizations.

For example, many of the components in a security policy created at a university may be appropriate for use at a large company. However, the same policy components may be too complex for a very small business or a nonprofit.

Creating and Enforcing Security Policies

Security policies should be based on the requirements of the organization. These requirements may be departmentally based or may vary across units within the organization.

An initial step in security policy creation is to collect and validate business requirements. The next step is to create components in the policy that successfully address each business requirement.

Once its security policy is in place, an organization must be able to enforce it. Effective enforcement starts with user training and awareness. Buy-in from employees is particularly important for policies to be successful. Additional methods include auditing and monitoring. Without enforcement and clear ramifications that result from policy breaches, a security policy becomes little more than a piece of paper.

Adaptability Is Key

Because the needs of an organization change over time, a security policy should remain adaptable to support changes as technologies change. In smaller environments, fluidity may exist, but resources may not be readily available to keep up with the implementation of a well-documented security policy. On the other hand, large organizations often have adequate resources but lack the flexibility of smaller entities.

You should review your security policies regularly to ensure that changes in technology haven't circumvented the policies, or require changes in the policies.

Parts That Make the Whole

All organizations—regardless of size or industry—have similar goals for achieving a more secure environment. A security policy helps secure the environment by documenting perceived risks and outlining mitigation plans. Security policies normally have multiple components, including the following:

- **Acceptable use policy:** This policy addresses network and Internet use as well as acceptable user behaviors and activities.

- **Enforcement policy:** This policy spells out how, when, and why security will be implemented in the environment, potentially including actionable consequences for breaching the policy.

- **Monitoring policy:** This policy specifies monitoring activities that are required. It also indicates who and what is monitored and at what frequency.

- **Physical access policy:** This policy specifies the physical resources to which users are granted access; it also includes information regarding the circumstances and mechanisms of authentication.

- **Educational policy:** This policy addresses the methods and frequency of user training.

The security policy might also address intrusion protection requirements, disaster recovery requirements, incident handling, authentication requirements, and more.

An Example of a Security Policy Outline

The following is an example of a simple security policy outline. If you don't already have a security policy in place, you could use this structure to get started. Just modify it for your organization:

1. Policy statement and introduction
   - General information
   - Objectives
   - Responsible organization structure
   - Security standards
2. Virus protection
3. Physical security
   - Definitions
   - Required security
4. Access controls
   - Authentication

5. Network and perimeter security

- Wired

- Wireless

- Firewalls and perimeter devices

6. Server security

- File server

- Web server

- Database server

- Print server

7. Workstation security

8. Mobile device security

9. Email systems

10. Telecommunication systems

11. Security services and procedures

- Auditing

- Monitoring

12. Computer security incident handling

13. Contacts and other resources

For each section of the outline, you need to fill in details that describe the security measures in your organization. However, your policy should not be so detailed that it becomes inflexible and difficult to update. The policy language should be clear and concise and must be understandable by all users.

You can find a wealth of sample security policy templates at the SANS Information Security Policy Templates website. Visit www.sans.org/security-resources/policies/.

A Closer Look at Acceptable Use Policies

Imagine that you're working on a team project and have some important deadlines approaching. One member isn't getting her work done on time but assures everyone that she's "on it." Every time you glance her way, she appears to be occupied. Finally, you walk past her desk and notice that she's on eBay, browsing auctions. At lunch you try talking to the team about the upcoming deadlines, but your coworker interrupts with "Did you see the dancing granny video on Facebook this morning? What a hoot!" You're fed up but not really sure what you can do.

The good news is that there may be a simple way to address this type of behavior. Most organizations create **acceptable use policies (AUPs)** that help managers enforce appropriate Internet usage.

An AUP outlines the rules of the road for accessing and using an organization's computing resources. To some of us, documenting acceptable computing activities and behaviors may seem like a reiteration of common sense. However, a surprising number of people abuse their privileges at work every day. A well-written AUP outlines appropriate usage and the consequences of disregarding the rules, including disciplinary actions that may be taken by an employee's manager.

In addition to using an AUP to regulate employee behavior, an organization might establish an AUP for legal protection. If an employee's behavior consists of a criminal act resulting in litigation, an AUP can help protect the employer. The AUP demonstrates that the organization did not support the employee's behavior. It establishes what is expected of employees and helps confirm that the employee was acting on his or her own accord, in violation of the policy.

In addition, organizations that create AUPs and require staff to follow them offer fewer opportunities for cybercriminals to exploit the environment and steal data. AUPs are designed to promote safe and appropriate user behavior, which greatly reduces the likelihood of legal proceedings that may result from data theft or other crimes. After all, business suffers when key employees are tied up fighting legal battles—unless you're an attorney!

What's In an AUP?

When an SME decides to establish an AUP as part of its security policy, the organization typically includes guidelines for using IT assets and performing computing activities. The AUP describes usage rules for systems and networks.

For example, the AUP may address web browsing, instant messaging, and checking email, providing examples of acceptable behavior. It may also describe role-specific activities—for example, for users, managers, and administrators. Or it may prescribe acceptable use for the entire user population, regardless of role.

Regularly remind users about AUP details using logon banners, routine training, and annual reviews with signed acknowledgments.

An AUP must also include the consequences of not adhering to the policy. Users must understand why they need to take an AUP seriously. With repercussions in place for violating the policy, the AUP becomes a much more formidable force. This is especially true in organizations where some users are transient. Universities, temp agencies, and companies that hire seasonal help have a significant number of users rotating in and out within a short time. The monitoring component of a security policy is especially critical in these organizations. Without monitoring, inappropriate user activity goes unnoticed. Also, with steeper repercussions and consistent enforcement, it's easier to encourage appropriate behavior.

The AUP should clearly state the consequences of breaching the policy. In addition, it's important that penalties are appropriate. For example, a user caught reading personal emails during work hours might receive a warning for a first offense; a user browsing pornography at work might be terminated. In many instances, the language of the AUP needs to be detailed and/or precise to properly address correct and incorrect behavior. Let's say your organization's AUP states that employees may not use Twitter. However, an IT employee follows a Microsoft Press author on Twitter to keep up to date on emerging technologies. In this case, a manager may be reluctant to discipline the employee. If the manager then disciplines someone else for personal Twitter use, the manager can be accused of inconsistent enforcement of the AUP.

In some cases of breach of the AUP, an organization's human resources department may need to get involved. Some situations may even be serious enough to involve the local authorities. Breaches of all sorts can happen in any organization, and it's important to be prepared for such situations. An AUP must be clearly written and thoroughly documented. It must also adhere to any local, state, and federal laws that apply.

An Example of an Internet Use Statement

The following is a portion of a sample Internet use statement that may be included as part of an AUP and could be further expanded to meet an organization's needs:

> Corporate assets are allowed to be used to access the Internet for business purposes only. Internet access from corporate equipment for non-business purposes is strictly prohibited. Accessing gaming sites, social networking sites (Twitter, Facebook, MySpace, and so on) for personal reasons, or pornographic or other sexually explicit materials on the Internet from corporate assets is strictly prohibited. Any Internet access that falls outside the bounds of business-specific behavior is considered a breach of policy. Failure to comply with this stated policy will lead to disciplinary action of the employee. Repeat offenses may lead to work suspension and possible termination of employment.

User Training

"I didn't know." These three simple words have led to severe security breaches in organizations large and small. User education and security awareness can stop most threats, including those launched by cybercriminals. A security policy is an organization's blueprint for safe computing. When it's followed, it acts like a shield against scammers. A policy stands a greater chance of success when everyone understands its importance and buys in to its terms. Employees need to understand why the policy is necessary, how to adhere to it, and what will happen if they don't. This is what security policy training is all about.

To get a security policy off the ground, management must agree that the policy is necessary. Then, managers must set an example by adhering to the policy.

Employees won't be interested in training that focuses only on consequences and penalties. They need to understand what can happen to the organization—and potentially their jobs—if a major security breach occurs. Presenting problems from their perspective can help you gain their support. It's also helpful to remind them that security can be very simple—that many security issues can be avoided by thinking before clicking.

Organizations change, and policies change, too. When changes occur, more training is needed. Therefore, an organization might consider offering security policy training in phases:

- Entry-level or introductory-level training for users who are new to the organization
- Periodic refreshers—perhaps quarterly or annually—to keep the users in touch with the security policy
- On-demand training as new scenarios or changes to the policy occur

Break Out the Surveys

Surveys can help ensure that users are learning from and supporting training efforts. You can ask users for feedback informally, such as through email or in person at the end of a session. Some organizations require employees to take a test or provide formal feedback at the end of training. An organization might keep training attendance, test results, and feedback as part of the employees' records. Regardless of the approach, you need a way to determine whether the training was effective.

Feedback can show you when you need to adapt training to meet the needs of any employees. Trainers can use feedback to improve and customize the training experience. Customized training leads to a more thorough understanding and adoption of the security policy.

Monitoring Techniques

After you've implemented a security policy, you need to ensure that it's having the desired effect. Ideally, you will want to validate all aspects of your security policy. This means that your validation and monitoring plan should not only include things such as checking for unauthorized access attempts into secured building areas but also recording and being alerted to unauthorized file access on the network.

To check on the state of your physical environment, you can conduct premises monitoring. **Premises monitoring** is the practice of monitoring multiple physical aspects of your environment. This may include but is not limited to areas such as:

- Parking lots

- Lobby and public waiting areas

- Unsecured employee areas, such as where receptionists or temporary workers are housed or conference rooms, cafeterias, and restrooms are located

- Secured employee work areas, such as an area where only authorized employees have been granted access

- Secured resource storage areas, such as datacenters and wiring closets

Why is physical security so important? Having physical access to a system gives an attacker a distinct advantage. For example, to access a network from the outside, an attacker has to traverse multiple firewalls, including network firewalls and host-based firewalls. Then he or she has to deal with authentication requests and prompts. If the attacker gets into the network, he or she might have to get past permissions configured on specific files and folders. However, acquiring physical access to a system on the network negates most of these protection mechanisms.

An attacker who gets physical possession of a system can boot the system from a CD or universal serial bus (USB) drive and then gain administrative access to the entire system. The attacker can then reset passwords, destroy or steal data, and format the system before moving on. An attacker may also choose to disrupt system activities by forcibly rebooting machines or installing undesired hardware or software such as keyloggers. Premises monitoring can help you prevent cybercriminals from accessing your systems.

A premises monitoring system may consist of multiple devices and monitoring systems, including the following:

- **Video cameras:** Before attackers can get to the computer systems in a data center, they must gain physical access to the building. Video cameras in parking lots and driveways allow you to track people entering the premises.

- **Door security:** To keep the systems in a facility secure, the doors to the facility must be secured. Often times when public access is granted to a facility, the entrance allows all visitors access to a sealed lobby area. Doors leading from the lobby to the user work areas and beyond are secured. Individuals who are allowed through those doors are admitted by a security guard or a technology such as card readers or key pads.

Do security guards or technologies provide better physical security? It depends. Certainly, it is possible for attackers to steal key cards or other credentials to bypass either type of security. However, when a security guard is responsible for granting access to the inside areas of a work environment, there is an increased chance of successful attacks using social engineering. An attacker might be able to sweet talk a night guard into granting access to a building, using a cup of coffee and a smile. Such tactics simply don't work with an access key pad.

Tracking User Activity and Behavior

Regularly reviewing access logs for sensitive areas can help an organization observe patterns of behavior. If a user repeatedly tries to gain access to the server room but his badge is denied access, this may be cause for concern. Similarly, an organization needs to keep track of who should have access to secure areas and who no longer needs it. For example, it's important to revoke access to secure locations once an employee leaves a department or the organization.

Something else to be aware of is **tailgating**. In environments that require card readers for door access, some users find it a nuisance to swipe their identification card in the reader every time they enter. So, employees start holding the door open for the person behind them. Tailgating is one of the primary access methods for unauthorized users, and social engineers use it all the time. Why wouldn't you hold the door for the guy wearing a delivery uniform? A social engineer simply waits for an authorized user to open and pass through a secure entry—and then follows right behind. Criminals rely on the polite tendency to hold the door for those behind us.

Educated users who respect and follow a security policy greatly reduce the opportunities available to social engineers and cybercriminals. As with most other security measures, user training is key. When they understand the rationale behind a policy—and understand the policy itself—users are more likely to comply. This compliance leads to safer, less vulnerable environments and fewer successful cybercrimes.

17

Protecting People and Assets with Security Technology

Network and security administrators work feverishly to protect their IT environments from attackers and other threats. Unfortunately, they have to set up mechanisms that protect from inside attackers (disgruntled employees, social engineers, and the like) as well as those on the outside.

In this chapter, you'll learn how to protect your IT environment and your employees with security technology.

Information Security Principles and Practices

Information security practices protect people and business assets from threats, including cybercriminals. The three key principles of confidentiality, integrity, and availability are commonly referred to as the CIA triad. Here's a quick look at each of these principles:

- **Confidentiality:** When properly achieved, confidentiality prevents unauthorized access to restricted data in an organization. An organization can enforce confidentiality by implementing access controls, such as authentication, and encryption.

- **Integrity:** An organization needs to validate that data, while in transit or at rest, has not been modified from its original state. Digital signatures and encryption help maintain data integrity.

- **Availability:** Data and access to data must be highly available and resistant to single points of failure. Data backups, redundant disks, and multiple network connections help ensure availability.

IT professionals can use many different methods to implement the CIA triad. Each organization must evaluate methods to select what's best for its environment.

Access Controls

To protect IT resources, such as servers, folders, and files, administrators can grant specific access, or permissions, to users and groups. This is accomplished through the use of access controls.

An **access control** is a system or technique for allowing or denying access. A door lock is a type of physical access control. Passwords and other types of identification and authorization, covered in Chapter 15, are also access controls. This section looks at controlling access through rights and permissions, in addition to physical controls.

An important concept surrounding access control is the **principle of least privilege**, which means giving users the least amount of access required for them to complete their jobs. By sticking to the most restrictive permissions required, you reduce the risk associated with mistakes (such as accidental deletions) and unwarranted access.

Overview of Permissions and Access Controls

Windows systems have two types of permissions: share permissions and NTFS permissions. Both permissions come into play when a user accesses a resource from a network. NTFS permissions also apply at the local level, on a user's PC. Share permissions are visible and configurable on the Sharing tab of a file or folder, and NTFS permissions are displayed on the Security tab.

Figure 17-1 shows the Security tab of a folder named Weekly Reporting Metrics. In the figure, SYSTEM and the Administrators group are the only entities with permission to the folder other the user who owns the folder. In this case, only default permissions have been applied to the folder. Typically, the owner of a resource (file, folder, hard drive, printer, and so forth) controls its permissions, as can administrators. Custom groups and additional individual users can be added to the access control list (ACL). Notice in Figure 17-1 that both Allow and Deny permissions are available.

In Figure 17-1, the owner of the folder is a user account called Administrator. This is different from the Administrators built-in group. The Administrators group represents multiple user accounts. All users who are part of the Administrators group have the indicated permissions simply because they are members of the group.

Cybercriminals usually don't have local access to a potential victim's computer or system. They attempt to break in through the network instead. Social engineers and

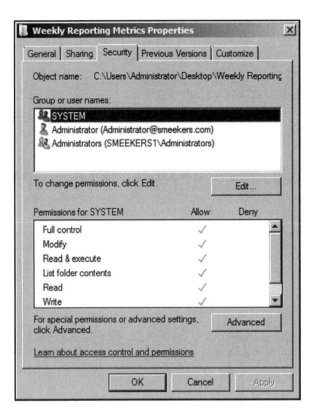

Figure 17-1
The NTFS permissions tab for a folder.

internal attackers often do get local access, and they can turn a local problem into a cyberincident. To prevent such incidents, you need to ensure that access controls are in place.

It's common to configure restrictive NTFS permissions rather than share permissions because NTFS permissions apply to both network and local access. If both share and NTFS permissions have been configured and the user accesses data from the network, the two permissions types are evaluated together to determine access rights. The more restrictive permission between the two takes effect.

For example, assume that a group named Human Resources has the Full Control share permission to a share named Background Checks. The group also has the NTFS Read permission on the same folder. Because Read is more restrictive than Full Control, any user whose account is a member of the Human Resources group will be granted only Read access to the Background Checks folder. Also, because the Read permission is configured at the NTFS level, it would apply regardless of the user access method. If the user connects from the network or locally on the computer that houses the resource, the resulting permission would be the same.

Restricting Electronic Access

When applying the principle of least privilege to electronic access, such as to computers and networks, you must understand what actions each user is required to perform.

Say that a folder named Background Checks exists on a server. The human resources (HR) and legal departments need access to the folder. The Human Resources group is responsible for adding newly completed background check files to the folder. Users in the Legal group only need to read the completed documents. By granting both groups Full Control of the folder, you have met their needs. However, the Legal group has a much higher level of permission than needed.

In this scenario, the users in *both* groups would be able to edit the files as well as delete files in the folder. Granting the excessive access creates an opportunity for user error—or even for intentional malicious destruction of data. The better course of action would be to grant the Legal group Read permissions only, while the Human Resources group would have Read and Write permissions.

Minimizing Use of Elevated Privileges

Systems administrators should use an ordinary user account for checking email, researching technologies, and other routine activities. The administrator-level account should be reserved for support and maintenance tasks that require more permissions.

Systems administrators require elevated privileges (that is, more permissions) to perform certain job functions. But this doesn't mean that all of their day-to-day activities require these rights. A user with elevated privileges who is logged in to a computer or the network introduces a vulnerability. If an attack takes over the login session, he or she may be able to exploit the higher-level permissions to do considerable damage.

The attack methods used to take over a session include social engineering, viruses, Trojan horses, and other types of malware. To mitigate this type of risk, administrators should practice the principle of least privilege.

Restricting Physical Access

It's important not to grant blanket physical access to secure locations in your organization. For example, consider a user whose primary role is database administration.

The server hosting the database is in a locked server room. The administrator connects to the database remotely to perform maintenance, so he never needs to physically enter the server room.

If the company has a blanket policy that grants all IT personnel access to the server room, the database admin would be included in that group. The end result is that a person who doesn't require access to a secure area to perform his job function has unnecessarily been granted access. This increases the chances for an attack. The database admin doesn't normally work in the server room, so he might not know the rules he must follow, and he could inadvertently allow a breach to occur.

Clear-cut Security Classifications

Classifying data is a way to label it for organizational purposes and to apply levels of security. One way to classify data is by access sensitivity. You first create broad security classifications (or categories) and then identify characteristics that qualify data for a particular label. Almost every government agency uses security classifications in some form. The following are some common government classification labels:

- Top secret
- Secret
- Confidential
- Restricted
- Unclassified

The same concept can be applied to business data. Classifications help administrators label data appropriately and help admins decide which users and groups should have access to the data. Every organization can establish its own set of security classifications. For instance, an organization might use the following data security classifications:

- Internal–Full access
- Internal–Restricted access
- External–Partner access
- External–Public access

The organization would need to define and clearly document each classification before putting it into practice.

Some small to medium enterprises (SMEs) use the government security classifications but modify them for their own environments.

Ideally, higher security classifications should be guarded more carefully. Additional security practices may be required to more carefully protect the data in these categories against cybercrime.

Separation of Duties

Separation of duties ensures that one person doesn't solely handle critical tasks. For example, the person who requests payment of an invoice in an organization should not be the same person signing the check. The goal of this separation is to prevent fraud and other illegal activities.

In IT, a software developer might separate operations from development and keep systems testing in yet another compartment. Doing so would reduce the risk of a tester, for example, making unauthorized changes or accessing operations data.

Another use of separation of duties in IT is to compartmentalize sensitive functions from non-sensitive ones and use different types of authentication for the two types of functions. Using access controls, an administrator would isolate a critical program and restrict the users or groups that have access to it. In addition, running the program would require a fingerprint scan and password or a token and password. This way, if an attacker wanted access to the program, he or she would need to jump through a few hoops:

- Break into the internal network.
- Learn the credentials of a user who has the appropriate permissions.
- Obtain the proper authentication credentials.

The odds are very low that an attacker will get through all these hoops, making the system very secure against breaches.

Separation of duties works well in all parts of an organization, from accounting to IT to HR. By determining which job responsibilities should not be intermingled, HR can work with hiring managers to plan appropriate job roles and responsibilities.

Regular Security Policy Audits, Updates, and Remediation

As computing environments change, security measures must change, too. In a busy environment, updating security controls and documentation can be back-burnered unintentionally. Regular security auditing is one way to get everything back on track.

An organization can work with internal departments or hire external companies that specialize in security auditing to perform the audits. It should schedule audits according to industry mandates, or at least annually. Both management and IT personnel should review the results of each audit.

Thorough audits point to security lapses, holes, and other weaknesses that can leave an SME vulnerable to attackers. An organization should fix any problems uncovered during an audit—to the extent that its budget allows. The organization may need to spring for technology updates, or it might be able to get away with just changing how employees use the existing assets.

After completing audits, an organization should review its security policies. It should update anything that's out of date or obsolete. Some SMEs must comply with federal or state regulations, so keeping security policies up to date may help avoid penalties as well as security breaches.

Many audits measure compliance with security policies. They help an organization determine if its security policies are just paper or actually followed.

Using Security Technology

The main purpose of security technology is to protect an entity against attackers and cybercriminals. Cybercrime offers monetary benefits, and frequent attacks against a network and its data are therefore common. The right mix of security technologies and methods can reduce your exposure.

Client-Side and Server-Side Security Considerations

Say that a user decides her locally installed firewall software is a nuisance, so she disables it. Because her computer is connected to the company network, which is protected by a network firewall, she believes nothing can go wrong with her system. Has she made an incorrect presumption? Does her action present a problem to other users and systems on the network? The short answer to both questions is yes.

One insecure computer in an environment may not seem like a big deal. But imagine if that computer became infected with a virus or a Trojan and then connected to the network. There is now the potential for a larger-scale security breach.

All clients (which may be workstations or mobile devices) and servers must be well protected. Antivirus software is critical to this strategy, as are firewalls and pop-up blockers. As another measure, lock down workstations and servers by disabling un-necessary services and protocols. If an attacker launches an attack using a service or protocol that isn't installed, the system is protected.

Tightly controlled authentication services, and server-specific rights and permissions like those associated with NTFS or Windows Active Directory, are also key. Administration of these components can often be centrally controlled, especially in larger SMEs; smaller organizations may prefer local system administration.

Public Key Infrastructure (PKI) and Kerberos

Some organizations use public key infrastructure (PKI) and Kerberos to provide strong authentication services. PKI is an infrastructure that uses authentication services and digital certificates to provide a high level of security. PKI uses two mathematically related cryptographic keys. The public key encrypts data, and the private key decrypts that data. The private key is very difficult for an attacker to calculate. The digital certificate provides reasonable assurance that the keys are valid.

Kerberos is a network security protocol that provides authentication and authorization services on a network. Kerberos uses strong cryptography for clients to prove their identity to a server. Once an identity is proven, the server encrypts the communication.

Securing the Networking Infrastructure

Most organizations value their data enough to protect it to some extent. Some organizations are more tuned in to security than others. Regardless of the security need, be it simple or extreme, the network plays a key part in achieving security goals.

In most organizations, all traffic to and from the Internet must flow through the network. Users access their data files and system resources over the network. Employees and business partners exchange email over the network. Voicemail may be retrieved over the network, and instant messages pass between users across the network. With all the functions made possible by a network, and because the network is a target for attackers, network protection must be strong.

Covering All the Access Points, Starting at the Perimeter

You typically enforce protection at different access points throughout a network. Starting at the perimeter, every network must have a firewall (see Figure 17-2). For instance, Internet traffic may flow in and out through a single router. This router should be enhanced or a firewall added to protect the network. The firewall can perform traffic inspection or even block specific access attempts.

Adding an intrusion detection system (IDS), intrusion prevention system (IPS), and web proxy server strengthens the security of the network perimeter. An IDS monitors network traffic and alerts administrators to possible malicious activity. An IPS goes a step further and may shut down network access when certain malicious activity is detected. Using an IDS or IPS enables you to observe threats, analyze them, and respond quickly.

Many solutions provide IDS and IPS functionality in a single device or software package. You can also deploy an IDS/IPS on workstations for added security.

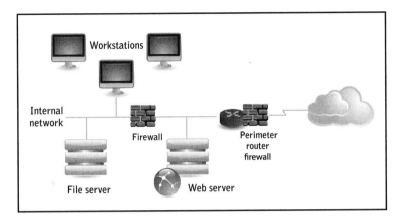

Figure 17-2
Protecting the network perimeter with a firewall.

A web proxy server enhances outbound security by filtering the websites that users are allowed to access. For example, if certain web domains are off-limits, the proxy server blocks those domains. Likewise, if certain types of content (video files, music files, and so on) are also off-limits, you can configure the server to block those types of file transfers or attachments.

You can configure a web proxy server (see Figure 17-3) to enforce the organization's acceptable use policy (AUP) as well as monitor traffic for restricted content. And you can implement an IDS and/or IPS to enhance inbound protection.

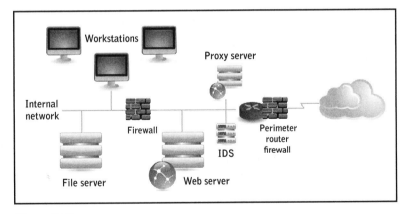

Figure 17-3
An IDS and web proxy server create a stronger perimeter.

Because network protection devices represent access points into the network, you need to consider their security. It's a good idea to require strong passwords on network devices and to encrypt connectivity between them.

Controlling Remote Access

Remote access is a sticky situation. You need offsite staff to be able to access the internal network. But by granting that access, you may be creating a weak spot in your network's security.

The safest way to allow remote access to an internal network is via a virtual private network (VPN), shown in Figure 17-4. You need a VPN server on your network (or a VPN server service running on an existing server), and you need VPN client software on the remote user's computer. You can even set up VPN access from a user's mobile phone.

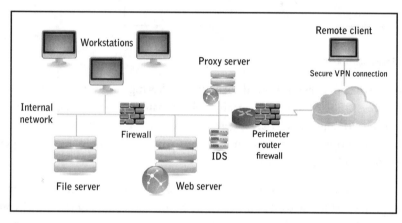

Figure 17-4
A VPN is an encrypted communication tunnel across the Internet.

Although a VPN provides safe passage over the Internet, there are still dangers to be aware of. If the client (computer or mobile phone) is infected with malware, the malware can spread to the internal network when the client connects. You should require that all clients connecting over a VPN have up-to-date antivirus protection. In addition, by enforcing strong passwords and multi-factor authentication, you reduce the number of ways cybercriminals can attack your system.

Establishing Virus-Free Conditions Throughout a Network

Antivirus software is crucial to any computing environment. Even with the best antispam and anti-phishing filters running on a mail server, bad stuff can still trickle through. It takes just one email with a malicious attachment and a clicky user to infect an entire network. To be more effective in identifying and controlling viruses, you need a layered approach.

An organization should install antivirus protection at the perimeter of a network and on individual workstations, as well as on servers. You want antivirus software at the perimeter because the perimeter network is an entry point from the public Internet. Many threats, including virus and malware propagation, originate on the Internet.

Perimeter devices, such as firewalls, web servers, and email servers, should all have antivirus software installed.

Even with the perimeter protected, you still need antivirus software on workstations. Users may unintentionally introduce viruses directly into the internal network. This may be accomplished with something as simple as a universal serial bus (USB) drive. Suppose a user took a file home to work on it at night. That home computer is infected by a virus, which spreads to the USB drive. The next day, when the user returns to the office with the USB drive, he plugs it into his computer and unwittingly spreads the virus to it. If his workstation doesn't have up-to-date local antivirus software, his computer may go on to infect other parts of the network.

We highly recommend VIPRE Business Antivirus and endpoint protection software from GFI. It won't slow down your PCs, and it scans your disks two to three times faster than other leading antivirus software.

Implementing Network Access Control and Management

Many SMEs have begun to use network access control mechanisms that allow them to police network entry points. Such systems allow an administrator to configure a ruleset that grants or denies access to the network. These systems often use health-checking software to evaluate a computer's state before the user is allowed to connect to the network. The health check may include validation tasks such as checking for operating system updates and verifying the presence of antivirus software and its update status. If a computer fails the health check, it may be isolated to a specific network segment or denied access altogether.

Say that Karen, a salesperson, arrives at your office for business. While waiting in the lobby, she boots up her laptop. Her laptop detects your company's wireless network, and she successfully connects to it. Unbeknownst to the IT group, Karen's antivirus software is long out of date and a worm is lurking on her computer. The malware now attempts to spread to your company's network.

If your company had a health-check solution in place, it would run a health check before allowing Karen's machine to connect. When the solution identified the worm on her system, it would either isolate her laptop or reject the connection attempt. Because you allowed a connection to occur before first validating the machine's state, you opened your network to exploitation.

Applying Patches and Security Updates

Because of the enormous amount of source code found in modern-day operating systems, applications, and web browsers, they're susceptible to bugs and security holes. Manufacturers release patches and updates whenever security problems are detected, or regularly. For example, Microsoft releases patches for the Windows operating system on the second Tuesday of every month—called Patch Tuesday—to help keep those systems safe from attackers.

Just as you can use tools to ensure antivirus software remains updated, you can also use tools to keep systems updated. Windows is configured by default to receive updates and service packs through the Windows Update feature automatically. When a workstation running Windows connects to the Internet, Windows Update scans the computer for high-priority updates including security updates, critical updates, and service packs. The service downloads the updates and installs them, as long as the computer is configured for automatic updates. Turning off the automatic updates feature puts a computer at high risk for malware infections and attack.

In network environments, you can also use Windows Server Update Services (WSUS) for patch management. WSUS centralizes and automates the management of Windows critical updates. Once you download updates to an WSUS management server, you test them to ensure they don't have unexpected effects on your network or applications. Then you can push them out to workstations at a time when network activity is low.

Firewalls, IDS/IPS solutions, and other networking devices require occasional updates also. Essentially, any device or application running on a network should be kept up to date to maintain the tightest security possible.

Sign up for security and technical alerts to stay on top of the latest threats. You can request Microsoft-related alerts and security bulletins by visiting the Microsoft Technical Security Bulletins website at http://technet.microsoft.com/en-us/security/dd252948.aspx. *Another good resource is the US-CERT Cyber Security Bulletins website at* www.us-cert.gov/cas/bulletins/.

18

Managing Online Banking Security Issues

In Chapters 7 and 9, we described a lawsuit filed by construction company Patco against its bank. The details of the lawsuit apply to this chapter as well. Patco alleged that the bank failed to maintain "reasonable security" over its online banking operations. As it happens, cybercrooks stole $345,000 of Patco's money because the bank didn't detect obvious fraudulent funds transfers.

This chapter discusses vulnerabilities that allow phishing-based attacks on bank accounts to succeed. It also discusses options for improving online banking security, which is why it appears in Part 3 of this book. Fraudulent funds transfers are an ongoing problem, and small to medium enterprises (SMEs) must be aware that online banking carries risks of fraud and theft.

As we were writing this chapter, we read a news flash about the OddJob Trojan, which targets online banking. This malware hijacks your online banking session and keeps the session (and account access) open even after you believe you've signed out. You don't even need to have the malware on your computer. In fact, just starting a new browser session can fire off a script that tells a control server to send a malware program your way, in real time. The criminals are getting more sophisticated—and scary.

As you work your way through this chapter, you'll learn about technical measures that can help prevent fraudulent funds transfers. But we see no magic bullets. Funds transfer security is a game of "cops and robbers." As soon as an attack is discovered and dissected, countermeasures are implemented. But then, a different attack comes along, and the game goes into another round.

In response to a 2009 security blog, well-known security company RSA (now the security division of EMC) posted this memorable statement:

> "Organizations that conduct business online should assume that all of their users' PCs are compromised in some manner and should prepare their security infrastructures accordingly."

We can't think of better security advice for organizations to ponder, then act upon!

Anti-Phishing Systems

Phishing is a known problem, and it always includes certain elements in its many forms. These include:

- The email origin being different from the reported or claimed origin
- An appeal for response
- A link to click (which takes the clicker to a destination of the cybercrook's choosing)

Why is there no technical solution to stop phishing attacks? This question is very interesting. Every major web browser includes anti-phishing elements, all the major security software packages include anti-phishing elements, and numerous technical solutions aim directly at phishing. Yet phishing attacks continue to succeed, despite all these security measures. How can this be?

On the banking side, phishing succeeds because many banks don't have or don't use sophisticated fraud-detection and prevention tools. Banking customers don't know this. Thus, most of them fail to use proper safeguards to make up for the bank's lack of fraud detection.

Phishing attacks continue to succeed because people keep falling for phishing emails, Tweets, and links on social network pages. As long as users keep clicking those poison links, some of them will lose money. That hasn't stopped software developers and financial institutions from attempting technical solutions to the problem of funds transfer fraud. Let's look at some of these solutions and determine why some have failed and others have succeeded to some degree or other.

The SiteKey Anti-Phishing System

SiteKey is a technology originally developed by Passmark, and acquired by RSA Security in 2006. It's an anti-phishing system that has been deployed at several giant financial institutions, including Bank of America and The Vanguard Group.

SiteKey depends on mutual authentication between users with online bank accounts and websites with bank account information. In this system, users identify themselves via login and other credentials to the banking website that has SiteKey running. The website then provides its own proof of identity to the end user, to demonstrate it is the real thing. Theoretically, mutual authentication means neither party can successfully be impersonated; both parties can be sure all communications are valid and legitimate.

When users establish a SiteKey login for their accounts, they first choose an image from a collection of thumbnail images. Next, users supply a title for that image, up to 30 characters long. Whenever a user logs into the site thereafter, after supplying an account name and passphrase for authentication, the site responds with the image and its title. The idea is to repeat the user's own data to "prove" that the site is real and not a phishing imposter site.

SiteKey adds another nice wrinkle to its behavior. It records the Internet Protocol (IP) address from which a user connects during SiteKey setup. If a user attempts to log in from a different IP address, even using valid SiteKey credentials, the system displays additional challenge-response questions to establish further proof of identity. Users pick three questions from a list of many options when they set up a SiteKey account, and they provide their own unique answers to those questions.

So why doesn't everybody adopt SiteKey and be done with it? SiteKey has weaknesses. In fact, it has enough weaknesses that SiteKey hasn't had any major adoptions since 2006. More telling, SiteKey no longer has much of a presence on the RSA security website. The problem is that a phishing site can steal the SiteKey information from a genuine site and then serve it up to users. Thus, a phishing site can "prove" its authenticity to the user and then steal the user's account information and, ultimately, money.

In addition, phishing victims whose PCs upload keylogs to cybercrooks may disclose everything needed to impersonate them on a legitimate SiteKey site anyway. When cyberthieves log in from a different IP address, they can supply the data from the key-log to get past the challenge-response hurdle.

In the end, SiteKey just doesn't cut it; it doesn't provide a secure or surefire means to foil phishing attacks. That's why it's no longer widely used or offered as an RSA product.

Anti-Phishing in Web Browsers

All the major web browsers—Microsoft Internet Explorer, Mozilla Firefox, Google Chrome, Opera, and Apple Safari—mention some kind of anti-phishing technology or another. For these browsers, the first line of defense is to check the validity of the digital certificate for websites that users visit. A **digital certificate** is a digital stamp that includes a very secure password issued by a reputable certificate authority, such as VeriSign or Thawte. Digital certificates are nearly impossible to forge, but they are relatively easy to steal. Because of the number of documented exploits involving stolen certificates, we consider them incomplete proof of valid website identity.

Microsoft's anti-phishing technologies include Sender ID Framework and the Internet Explorer Phishing Filter. (Internet Explorer 8 uses similar functionality that goes by the name SmartScreen.) Although the major web browsers don't handle phishing in exactly the same way, Microsoft's approach is representative enough to explain why browsers by themselves can't completely counter phishing attacks.

Sender ID is a Microsoft-sponsored industry initiative for email authentication. It verifies the domain name from which an email is sent. If a lookup returns a different value from what the email contains, the message is assumed to be fraudulent and gets discarded. This initiative also uses Sender Policy Framework (SPF) records to identify and authenticate legitimate email messages.

A quick look at spam statistics from Spam Arrest (see Figure 18-1) illustrates why this initiative has neither done away with spam nor stopped phishing in its tracks. In this figure, the line just above the X-axis in the line graph represents SPF messages as a percentage of all emails received. It shows that only 10%–15% of messages use SPF records. Simply put, SPF isn't used widely enough to make much difference.

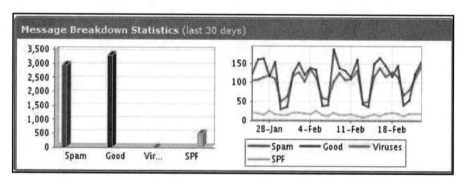

Figure 18-1
Spam statistics from Spam Arrest.

Microsoft's Phishing Filter combines client-side filtering to block bad sites with "up-to-the hour information on the latest reporting phishing websites from both end users and 3rd party data sources." Unfortunately, more than 50% of all victims are caught within the first hour after a phishing site goes up. Reporting and blacklisting known bad sites occurs too slowly to keep up with phishing attacks. By the time a site gets listed, it has already phished most of its victims!

Blacklisting *is a way to block spam email. If an Internet service provider (ISP) blacklists a particular email server, any emails sent from that server to the ISP are automatically discarded.*

About.com ranks the Netcraft Anti-Phishing Toolbar better than those for Internet Explorer and Firefox. (Opera and Microsoft license Netcraft's anti-phishing data, which makes this ranking puzzling. On the face of it, IE and Netcraft should earn the same ranking.) The Netcraft toolbar is a community-based reporting initiative that weights reports from expert or highly trusted users more highly than those with low reporting frequency or history. Although this approach may produce better results, it's still too slow to catch everything. The tool does report online reputation scores for the sites that users visit, however, which can provide warning about suspect or malicious sites.

Online Reputation

Online reputation is a method for assessing the credibility of websites, sellers, writers, information providers, and other online players and personalities. Numerous vendors offer online reputation systems. These systems assign numeric values or rankings to assessments. They incorporate ratings from users or buyers, as well as information about spam, malware, and spyware reported for specific sites and addresses. Most Internet security software systems provide reputation scores for websites users seek to visit. This is intended to help steer them away or wave them through to those sites.

Hundreds of anti-phishing software tools, browser add-ins, and uniform resource locator (URL) filtering services are available on today's market. Yet phishing remains real, present, and chronic. Microsoft notes in its discussion of phishing that another key ingredient in avoiding phishing attacks is user education. This area is in urgent need of attention and information. It alone explains why phishing attacks continue to succeed, despite all the money and technology thrown at the problem. Simply put, users keep falling for lures in phishing attacks and keep clicking suspect links! As long as that keeps up, at least some phishing attacks are bound to succeed.

More on Trusteer Rapport

In Chapter 6, we introduced a browser add-in called Rapport from Trusteer. It works by acting on a PC's runtime environment whenever users access any designated websites. In practice, this means the software kicks in only when a user accesses a password-protected website. At that point, Rapport steps in to block local behaviors that might compromise online security. Some users (including your author) might find this too restrictive for an ordinary user account.

Here's a list of measures Rapport takes to prevent security breaches or lapses that might aid cybercrooks in data harvesting and phishing attacks:

- **Blocking keyloggers and screencaps:** Keylogger Trojans record keystrokes or make screen captures whenever specific activity occurs on their host systems. Financial activity of any kind usually triggers this behavior. Rapport blocks such behavior and alerts users if it occurs while they're visiting a Rapport-protected site. (There's a server-side piece to this software, too, that protects the other side of online banking interactions.) Rapport also encrypts keyboard data before it hits the network. This enforces local security on the PC and prevents keylogging before keystrokes are handed off to Secure Sockets Layer (SSL).

- **Preventing man-in-the-middle or redirection attacks:** Rapport uses delivery confirmation for financial and other Rapport-protected websites. This prevents attackers from mounting man-in-the-middle attacks, bogus redirection, and other phishing techniques. It also prevents hijacking of live online banking sessions. Rapport succeeds in verifying that the site a user wants to access is actually being accessed—and not some other site.

- **Foiling phishing and social engineering scams:** Rapport tags all sensitive user data and associates it with legitimate sites where it may be safely and properly used. Anytime the software detects use of such information for another site, it halts communication and warns the user. Only if the user specifically allows such use will that tagged information be sent to other sites.

The combination of a Rapport client on the user side and Rapport server software at the online banking site appears to offer the best hope for foiling fraudulent funds transfers available today. As more banks start providing Rapport's client to work with their Rapport-enhanced server installations, online banking will become much more secure.

Rapport already sounds pretty good to most users and to a lot of banks. As we write this chapter, Rapport has been downloaded nearly 19 million times.

There are some downsides to working with Rapport, however. It does restrict the functionality of the user desktop while a web browser is running. (And that's most of the time that people use their computers these days.) Rapport can also slow Internet access because of the extra layers of software it uses to provide additional security.

We recommend that those who use Rapport set up a special, limited-access user account on their PCs strictly for online banking. Then they should install Rapport only for that account. The security trick is to make sure all online banking activity occurs only when logged in to the limited-access account.

Man-in-the-Middle, Bogus Redirection, and Session Hijacking

A man-in-the-middle attack involves intercepting traffic in both directions for an ongoing connection and then relaying all data sent and received between the two parties. The proverbial man in the middle (the attacker) can record, read, or even alter the contents of that traffic. Such attacks are easily foiled with address verification because both sides must interact with the attacker, rather than each other, for this attack to work.

Bogus redirection captures traffic addressed to a legitimate site and sends (redirects) it to a different site instead. Some malware does automatic redirection to fool users into thinking they're interacting with a valid and legitimate site rather than a malicious one. Here again, address verification easily foils this type of attack.

Session hijacking is an attack method that captures the attributes of a session from one of the parties involved (usually on the client or user end). It then takes over (hijacks) the session from the legitimate user. The attacker keeps the session going and impersonates the user. The user usually blames an Internet hiccup for an apparently lost or broken session and simply reconnects through another session. Ongoing connection validation is needed to detect hijacking. Rapport also supports this capability and breaks any hijacked sessions within seconds of such an attack.

19

Fostering Internet Security Awareness

"The Internet is the crime scene of the 21st Century." That quote by Manhattan District Attorney Cyrus Vance, Jr., in an October 2010 *Wall Street Journal* article, sums up the high-tech and global state of crime on the Internet today.

International organized cybercrime is thriving. Web-based crimes are easy to commit, and they rake in hundreds of millions of dollars annually. The bad guys come up with more and better ways of victimizing us every day. Protections that worked well last year or last month may be useless today, leaving your organization at high risk of data theft and financial loss. Small to medium enterprises (SMEs) need to be as vigilant as large corporations in keeping the criminals at bay.

This chapter spotlights the most effective means of combating cybercrime: security awareness. You'll learn what it entails, how it can make or break an SME, and how training can help your organization maintain the upper hand in the fight against cybercrime.

What Is Internet Security Awareness?

The aim of **Internet security awareness**, or cybersecurity awareness, is to teach people web-based safety techniques and provide a strong shield against cybercrime. Technology provides a lot of protection. Antivirus and antispyware software monitors emails and web surfing sessions, filtering out a large amount of cybercrud. Network and computer firewalls do a good job keeping outsiders from becoming insiders. Access controls help ensure that only authorized users can use network resources. But no technology protection is perfect.

Cybercriminals come up with new ways to bypass technology guards all the time. In addition, malware evolves rapidly, and phishing gets more sophisticated each month. Only by understanding threats to computers and data while surfing the Web (or checking email, instant messaging, or texting) can we learn to avoid becoming victims.

Crackers and other cybercriminals release 70,000 new malware variants every day and send 800 million spear-phishing emails. The numbers just keep going up and up.

This book has detailed the cyberthreats you and your employees are likely to encounter. Many things that seem like simple annoyances—spam, email, and pop-up ads in particular—are vehicles for potentially dangerous phishing scams and drive-by downloads. A scammer can steal your organization's identity, open credit accounts, and run up thousands of dollars of fraudulent purchases. A drive-by download may silently install keylogger software that then captures user names, passwords, and other private information. By the time you uncover such problems, it's usually too late: You or your organization will suffer a financial loss, as well as a blow to your reputation if the crime goes public. In severe cases, where the losses are too great or regulatory compliance is breached, organizations fold.

Most SMEs provide some type of sexual harassment training during new employee orientation or annually for all employees. Yet 79% of SMEs have no formal policy or security awareness training program in place.

Don't let this happen to your organization. Help your employees recognize phishing emails and scam advertisements. Teach them what to do and what not to do when presented with suspicious messages and links. Security awareness is the essential counterstrike against cybercriminals, and it's the key to avoiding those crimes in almost every case. For the best protection, make Internet security awareness training an essential part of your defense-in-depth strategy and require training for all employees.

National Cyber Security Awareness Month (NCSAM)

October is National Cyber Security Awareness month. Since 2004, this public awareness campaign has encouraged home users, businesses, schools, nonprofits, and government agencies to "protect their computers, children, and data." Driven in part by the National Cyber Security Alliance (NCSA), the organization wants Internet users to understand the impact their online behavior has on web security as a whole and to share the responsibility for making the Web a safer place.

About Internet Security Awareness Training (ISAT)

ISAT teaches participants safe surfing and messaging habits. SMEs should encourage ISAT for employees to avoid the fallout from cybercrimes. Training helps employees avoid failures and may reduce or eliminate your organization's liabilities in lawsuits. In addition, employees who have taken ISAT generally feel more confident about meeting threats head on. They might also come out of training with a better attitude toward your organization's security policy—a win–win for everyone.

Organizations that are regulated—for example, by the Sarbanes-Oxley Act or the Payment Card Industry Data Security Standard (PCI DSS)—require employees to take ISAT at least annually to meet compliance requirements. Many states also require state-owned educational institutions to provide ISAT for all users.

SMEs can offer free or low-cost ISAT in a variety of ways. Easy, any-organization-can-do-it training may include the following:

- **Email alerts:** Send weekly or monthly cybersecurity emails with safety tips and maybe a link to a current news article about a security breach.

- **Newsletter or intranet articles:** If you produce an in-house newsletter or have an intranet, regularly include articles on the latest threats.

- **Brown bag lunch seminars:** Lunchtime seminars work well for busy staff members who already have too much email to sift through. Cover the most important security information in a one-hour session and then schedule staff for more in-depth training when their workload permits.

The next step up is online training. Formal, professional courses are usually the best ISAT option. An in-depth, immersive course experience has a lasting effect on most participants.

Benefits of Online ISAT

For many SMEs, training isn't a core business function. Training is necessary, but the development, management, and delivery of training can pull a manager away from more pressing tasks. In addition, a learning management system (LMS) can be a major upfront investment and requires time and effort to maintain. If you choose online training packages offered by a third party, you don't need in-house staff and other resources to deliver the training. For a reasonable fee, your employees can get detailed training through on-demand webinars, letting them attend courses as their schedules allow. Even remote employees, whether in another city or another country, are easily included; all they require is an Internet connection.

In addition, online training companies provide course outlines. You know exactly which topics are covered and in what detail, ensuring that all employees receive the same information. Some training companies are willing to customize their courses for your organization's unique needs.

Some ISAT course providers offer onsite training, either at the client's facility or the training provider's facility.

Typical ISAT Course Topics

Not every ISAT course is the same, so you should compare course outlines carefully before selecting a training partner. Topics typically covered in ISAT courses include the following:

- What cybercrime is and how it continues to thrive
- How cybercrime reaches its targets through malware, phishing, and social engineering
- How to protect sensitive information on computers
- Why security policies, which include password policies and acceptable use policies, are important
- How failing to adhere to policies affects organizations (for example data theft, financial losses, diminished reputation, legal proceedings) and employees (for example reprimands, terminations)

Now that you know what to expect from ISAT courses, let's take a look at KnowBe4's training program.

KnowBe4 Security Awareness Training

Traditional security awareness training is static, and it's sometimes developed by HR or department managers rather than IT security specialists. Those trainers update courses annually or less often. In today's cybercrime climate, that's not often enough.

KnowBe4 specializes in IT security. KnowBe4's team of security and e-learning specialists provide state-of-the-art courseware (see Figure 19-1) that's relevant to individuals, SMEs, and large corporations. Plus, KnowBe4 uses Dynamic Content Updates (DCU) technology to update its First2Know Internet Security Awareness Training every day, describing threats your employees may encounter on the Web now.

Figure 19-1
First2Know ISAT is delivered on demand, over the Internet.

KnowBe4's comprehensive security awareness training program helps you and your employees identify and prevent IT security incidents. Its program includes the following:

- Annual Internet security awareness training
- On-demand refresher training for all employees
- Ongoing Phishing Security Tests, which are simulated phishing attacks, so you know the percentage of end users who are Phish-prone™
- Training history reports for regulatory compliance
- Free ThreatApp™, a smartphone app that sends daily messages about current phishing attacks
- Security awareness posters for your office or facility
- A security awareness screensaver that includes your company logo

Courseware

KnowBe4 training modules are designed to be effective and engage participants without overwhelming them with information (see Figure 19-2). A typical module lasts 20 to 25 minutes. If you need to stop a training session temporarily, the software remembers where you left off. When you return, you can begin from that point.

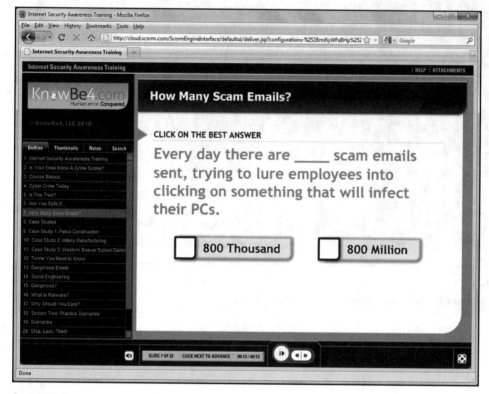

Figure 19-2
The First2Know ISAT modules are user friendly and engaging.

Built-in scenarios quiz participants about topics covered in the module (see Figure 19-3). The quizzes are designed to reinforce important cybersafety concepts, and they encourage critical thinking in real-world situations.

No special equipment is needed for First2Know training. Participants simply need an Internet connection and can use any web browser that supports Adobe Flash.

Reporting

KnowBe4 provides courseware-related reports to managers and project leaders. You'll receive statistics on enrolled employees, their status, completion, and many other parameters.

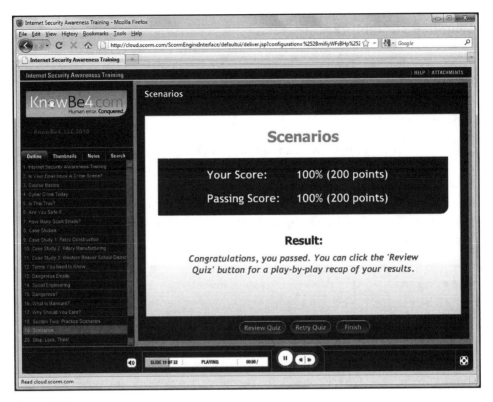

Figure 19-3
Participants get immediate feedback on quiz results and can review their work before continuing.

Pricing

KnowBe4 offers competitive training rates. For an average 200-seat organization, your annual subscription is about $7 per seat. Larger organizations get tiered volume discounts that may bring those prices even lower.

ThreatApp

ThreatApp is a free service provided by KnowBe4 that sends an update to your smartphone regarding a threat that's hot that day. You can download this app from the *KnowBe4.com* website.

ThreatApp reminds you to stay alert and think before you click a link in an email or on a website. The service is a great way to reinforce ISAT.

KnowBe4 Phishing Security Tests

KnowBe4 recently performed a Phishing Security Test (PST) for a customer prior to training. This test involved sending a simulated phishing attack to its employees. A whopping 21% of recipients responded to the email. We refer to those employees as *Phish-prone*. The Phish-prone percentage of your organization provides justification for employee ISAT.

PSTs are also used to reinforce training and check its effectiveness. Upon completion of KnowBe4 training, participants will receive simulated phishing attacks. Employees who fall for an attack will receive an online training reminder as a corrective measure to help them get back on track. Managers and project leaders benefit from the results of the simulated attacks by understanding additional training needs and their organization's overall security compliance.

Employees who fail a simulated attack and receive remedial training are 50% less likely to get fooled again in later attacks.

Consulting Services

KnowBe4 can help you plan and implement a security awareness training program. And you don't need to replace a training program you already have in place. KnowBe4 courses are SCORM 2004 compliant. That means we can deliver courseware for your in-house learning management system, if needed. We also offer competitive upgrade discounts to help you supplement your current training program.

How to Contact KnowBe4

Visit the *KnowBe4.com* website to learn more about our programs and services. You can also contact us as follows:

- Send an email to *info@KnowBe4.com*

- Call 855-KNOWBE4 (566-9234)

Appendix A
Acronyms and Glossary

List of Acronyms

ACH: Automated Clearing House

ACL: access control list

AP: access point

AUP: acceptable use policy

B2B: business-to-business

BBB: Better Business Bureau

CEO: chief executive officer

CFO: chief financial officer

CIA: confidentiality, integrity, and availability

CTR: currency transaction report

CVN: card verification number

DCU: Dynamic Content Updates

DDoS: distributed denial of service

DoS: denial of service

EFT: electronic funds transfer

FBI: Federal Bureau of Investigation

FDIC: Federal Deposit Insurance Corporation

FTC: Federal Trade Commission

HR: human resources

HTML: Hypertext Markup Language

HUD: Housing and Urban Development

IC3: Internet Crime Complaint Center

IDS: intrusion detection system

IP: Internet Protocol

IPS: intrusion prevention system

IRS: Internal Revenue Service

ISAT: Internet security awareness training

ISP: Internet service provider

IT: information technology

LMS: learning management system

NCSAM: National Cyber Security Awareness Month

NW3C: National White Collar Crime Center

PBX: private branch exchange

PIN: personal identification number

PO: purchase order

SAR: suspicious activity report

SME: small to medium enterprise

SMS: Short Message Service

SMTP: Simple Mail Transfer Protocol

SPF: Sender Policy Framework

SSL: Secure Sockets Layer

URL: uniform resource locator

USB: universal serial bus

VoIP: voice over Internet Protocol

VPN: virtual private network

Glossary

access control   A system or technique for allowing or denying access. A door lock is a type of physical access control. Passwords and other types of identification and authorization are also access controls.

active content   Program code inside one or more objects on a web page. When a web browser accesses a page with active content, the code is automatically downloaded and executed on the user's PC.

advance-fee fraud   A type of scam in which a cybercriminal persuades a potential victim to help transfer a substantial amount of money to an account. The victim is offered a commission for facilitating the transaction or multiple transactions. The Nigerian scam, also called the 419 scam, is a prime example of advance-fee fraud.

application whitelisting   Allowing only known software to execute within an organization's computing systems.

authentication   The process of identity verification, which can take a number of forms. A user name and password combination is a simple form of authentication.

Automated Clearing House (ACH)   An electronic network that banks and other financial institutions use to conduct transactions. These transactions use information found on business and consumer checks, normally authorized by that organization or consumer. The transfer might be a single or recurring debit to their account.

blacklisting   A way to block spam email. If an Internet service provider (ISP) blacklists a particular email server, any emails sent from that server to the ISP are automatically discarded.

bogus redirection   A process that captures traffic addressed to a legitimate website and sends (redirects) it to a different website instead. Some malware does automatic redirection to fool users into thinking they're interacting with a valid and legitimate site rather than a malicious one.

botherder   See *botmaster*.

botmaster   The malicious person in charge of a botnet.

botnet   A network of remotely controlled computers, usually meant for malicious purposes.

challenge-response sequence   A form of identity validation in which a user must answer a set of questions that only he or she knows the answers to.

clear text   Unencrypted text sent over a network, such as the Internet, that can be read by anyone who captures the transmission.

con man   Short for "confidence man," a swindler who gains a person's trust or confidence for the purpose of fraud. Once trust is gained, a fraudster can more easily take the victim's money.

cybercrime   Crime committed using an Internet-connected computer.

cyberheist   Another term for cybercrime.

dark figure of crime   The amount of crime that remains undiscovered and unknown.

defense in depth   A network protection strategy that uses multiple layers of security.

denial of service (DoS) attack   Overloading a computer with so much traffic or requests that communications to and from that computer are disrupted. Attackers often launch DoS attacks against web servers, preventing anyone else from accessing the associated websites.

digital certificate   A digital stamp or electronic document that verifies the identity of a person or organization. The certificate includes a very secure password issued by a reputable certificate authority, such as VeriSign or Thawte.

distributed denial of service (DDoS) attack   An extension of a DoS attack in which several systems are used to deploy an attack. Using many systems for a DDoS attack can ensure that communications are completely denied rather than disrupted to a lesser extent.

drive-by download   A transfer of software from a web server to an unsuspecting user's computer. It occurs in the background, with no notification, when a user visits a particular web page. A user need only access the web page to be subject to the download. Such downloads usually include malware when some kind of scam or attack is under way.

encryption   The process of making clear text unreadable. Before anyone can read encrypted text, it must first be decrypted. By encrypting sensitive data, you greatly reduce opportunities for criminals to steal sensitive information.

firewalls   Hardware devices or software that restrict the types of traffic that may flow into, through, and out of an internal network.

follower   A Twitter user who subscribes to another Twitter user's Tweets. Followers see Tweets from these subscriptions on their own home page.

fraud   The criminal act of misleading and misdirecting a victim through trickery.

harvest   To acquire data illicitly. The data is usually some form of credentials, such as account names or numbers, passwords, and challenge-response sequences. An unauthorized third party—usually, a cyberthief—often uses the information to impersonate the individual or organization whose credentials have been stolen.

heuristic detection   A method of malware detection that doesn't depend on knowing the specific signature characteristics of a known type of malware. Heuristic methods look for more generic elements of programs that are indicative of viruses or other malware rather than those types of software that are expected to be found on computers.

Internet security awareness   The ability to recognize Internet-based threats, such as phishing emails and scam advertisements, and how to safely avoid them.

keylogger   Malware that records every keypress a user makes on his or her machine into a special file called a keystroke log.

malware   Any software that's installed on a computer with the intention of executing malicious code and/or causing damage. Typically, the software installs without the owner's permission.

man-in-the-middle attack   An attack in which data sent and received between two parties in an ongoing connection is intercepted. The attacker can record, read, or even alter the contents of that traffic.

money mule   A person recruited by a criminal or criminal organization to quickly receive and turn around funds involved in scams. The scams are often related to ACH, credit card, or similar online transactions. The money mule is often unaware of his or her actual role.

multi-factor authentication   A method of validating the identity of a user by using two or more security mechanisms. For example, a valid user name and password combination along with a fingerprint scan is a form of multi-factor authentication.

Nigerian scam   A fraud often perpetrated via email in which a scamster promises financial gain in return for funds advanced. The scam began in the 1980s, at the decline of a once oil-based Nigerian economy. Dozens of variations now exist throughout different countries. Also called the 419 scam.

one-factor authentication   A method of validating the identity of a user by a single credential or set of credentials. A valid user name and password combination is a form of one-factor authentication.

online reputation   A ranking system for assessing the credibility of websites, sellers, writers, information providers, and other online players and personalities.

packet analyzer   See *sniffer*.

phishing   Email fraud that uses various techniques to persuade someone to divulge sensitive or confidential information, such as credit card or bank information. Phishing is a kind of social engineering attack.

phone number harvesting   Gathering cellphone or voice over Internet Protocol (VoIP) numbers for advertising purposes, to make unauthorized calls, or for other deceptive purposes.

phrase techniques   Methods of producing strong passwords. One technique involves creative transformations for a sentence so that, for example, "I never eat rye bread" becomes iN3V3RtaeWRYdearb.

phreaking   A form of fraud that involves directly hacking telecommunications systems.

principle of least privilege   Giving users the least amount of access required for them to complete their jobs.

protocol analyzer   See *sniffer*.

proxy server   A computer or an application that acts as an intermediary for requests between a client workstation and a server. A common use of proxy servers is to cache web pages or files that are frequently requested. Providing the cached pages reduces network traffic.

rogueware   Spyware or other malware that often masquerades as antivirus software. Users respond to bogus virus discovery pop-up ads or repair offers to help them get rid of viruses they don't really have. Instead, malware is installed on their machines.

safe computing   The application of safeguards and precautions that protect you from becoming a victim of computer crimes, especially cybercrime.

safe surfing   A user's cautious behavior when browsing the Web.

security policy   A written document that states how an organization plans to protect its physical assets and information.

separation of duties   Ensures that one person doesn't solely handle critical tasks.

session hijacking   An attack method that captures the attributes of a website session from one of the parties involved (usually on the client or user end). It then takes over (hijacks) the session from the legitimate user. The attacker keeps the session going and impersonates the user.

Simple Mail Transfer Protocol (SMTP)   An Internet standard used for sending and receiving email.

smishing   Phishing conducted via Short Message Service (SMS), a telephone-based text messaging service. A smishing text, for example, attempts to entice a victim into revealing personal information.

sniffer   A network tool that captures data transmitted across a cable or wireless connection and lets the user analyze the data to determine its payload. Also referred to as a *packet analyzer* or *protocol analyzer.*

social engineering   The act of tricking people into divulging information that they shouldn't share with an unauthorized third party. Also, the act of gaining sensitive information by deception.

social media   The platforms, or channels, used for social networking. Examples of communication channels are Facebook, Twitter, blogs, and YouTube.

social networking   Actively engaging in online conversations with other people or groups of people. Communication is multidirectional because social networking is all about connecting, collaborating, and sharing information freely.

spam   Unsolicited, junk email usually sent in massive broadcasts.

spear phishing   A type of phishing attack that aims to collect information about a specific organization or company. Spear-phishing messages may appear to originate from a large or well-known company or website, a coworker, or an internal manager.

spoofing   Forging an email header so that the message appears to have originated from someone other than the actual source.

steganography   The art or practice of hiding digital information within messages or images.

tabnabbing   Using browser tabs to impersonate legitimate websites and create fake login pages that trick victims into revealing private information. Tabnabbing works when you have two or more tabs open in a web browser. When a tab is left unattended for several minutes, a tabnabber can redirect the site in the unattended tab to a different, malicious login site.

tailgating   A method used by social engineers to gain access to a building or other protected area. A tailgater waits for an authorized user to open and pass through a secure entry and then follows right behind.

Trojan (or Trojan horse)   Malware that sends information from a victim's computer to a remote computer, usually across the Internet, for malicious purposes. When used with a keystroke logger, the Trojan sends the keylog to cyberthieves who comb the log for sensitive user information.

Trusteer Rapport   A browser add-in program that increases anti-phishing protection in most modern web browsers. It locks down web browsers, checks to make sure that websites use authentic current digital certificates, blocks drive-by downloads, and helps prevent online fraud.

typosquatting   Purchasing a web domain that is a character or two different from a legitimate and well-known social or company website. When a person mistypes the web address, a website appears that looks very much like the intended site. Typosquatting is usually done for fraudulent purposes. Also called *URL hijacking*.

URL shortening   A method of reducing the size and complexity of web URLs, mainly for ease of use. However, URL shortening also disguises a website's real domain name, and hinders detection of known malicious sites or destinations.

vishing   A phishing attack conducted by telephone, usually targeting voice over IP (VoIP) users, such as Skype users.

voicemail overloading   Spamming over Internet telephony. Much like getting spam email, a voice over Internet Protocol (VoIP) user can get junk voicemails. Spammers simply send a voicemail message to thousands of IP addresses at a time.

whaling   Phishing attacks that target high-ranking executives at major organizations or other highly visible public figures.

zombie   Compromised computers that form a botnet.

Appendix B
Resources

This appendix lists several cybercrime- and security-related resources aimed at small to medium enterprises (SMEs), many of which are included in this book.

Banking Security

Bank Info Security
www.bankinfosecurity.com/

This news site is chockfull of articles related to financial fraud, data breaches, and security compliance. Sign up for the e-newsletter or register with the site to get breaking news alerts and cyber advisories delivered to your inbox.

Your Money Is Not Safe in the Bank!
http://yourmoneyisnotsafeinthebank.org/

This site takes a blunt look at the safety of commercial banking accounts, and provides numerous articles about banking-related crimes against businesses. It's run by the Cyber Looting Awareness & Security Project (CLASP), a group of cybercrime victims who believe that "online banking should be safe for businesses as well as individuals."

Credit Card Security

Payment Card Industry (PCI) Security Standards Council
www.pcisecuritystandards.org/smb

The PCI Security Standards Council site provides detailed guidance on cardholder data security. Any organization that accepts credit or debit cards as payment for goods or services should already be highly familiar with this website.

Visa Security Sense
www.VisaSecuritySense.com

Aimed at consumers and organizations, this site provides tips for protecting cardholder security, preventing fraud, and more. The Fraud News and For Retailers sections are good resources for SMEs.

General Scam/Fraud Information and Security

Better Business Bureau
www.bbb.org

The Resource Library at *www.bbb.org/us/Business-Resources/* includes an Alerts link that describes recent scams and marketplace issues. You may also browse the Data Security – Made Simpler pages at *www.bbb.org/data-security/* for general security information, or download and read the Security & Privacy – Made Simpler guide from *www.bbb.org/us/corporate-engagement/security/*.

Computer Crime Research Center
www.crime-research.org/

A collection of news feeds, articles, and forums based on computer crime, Internet fraud, and cyberterrorism. The site is run by a nonprofit, non-governmental, scientific research organization.

Consumer Fraud Reporting (CFR)
www.consumerfraudreporting.org/

This website is aimed at consumers but is a great resource for SMEs too.

Microsoft Technical Security Notifications
http://technet.microsoft.com/en-us/security/dd252948.aspx

You can sign up for Microsoft-related alerts and security bulletins at this website.

SecurityWeek
www.securityweek.com

This well-known and respected weekly magazine is a first-stop for many SMEs looking for the latest business security news.

StaySafeOnline.org
http://staysafeonline.org

The For Business section includes tips for protecting your organization, employees, and customers from cyber-related crime.

Government Agencies

Federal Bureau of Investigation (FBI) Cyber Crime
www.fbi.gov/about-us/investigate/cyber/cyber

The FBI's Cyber Crime section of the official website offers information and intelligence aimed at the public and private sectors worldwide.

Federal Deposit Insurance Corporation (FDIC)
www.fdic.gov

The FDIC website provides information on banking industry regulations, bank closures, statistics, and analyses. Special alerts (SAs) notify the public of banking-related scams and issues. You can sign up by email or RSS to get SAs sent to you, or just visit the Special Alerts section of the website periodically.

Federal Trade Commission (FTC)
http://ftc.gov/

The FTC provides information to help consumers spot and avoid fraudulent practices in the marketplace. The Privacy & Security section (*http://ftc.gov/bcp/menus/consumer/tech/privacy.shtm*) offers tips that are useful to SMEs and their employees, too.

The FTC Bureau of Consumer Protection Business Center at *http://business.ftc.gov/* offers a plethora of information for SMEs related to fraud protection, privacy issues, and complying with regulations.

Internet Crime Complaint Center (IC3)

www.ic3.gov/default.aspx

The IC3 is a joint partnership between the FBI and the National White Collar Crime Center (NW3C). The organization receives cybercrime complaints and reports statistics, acting as a central referral system for law enforcement and regulatory agencies. The IC3 also provides the annual *Internet Crime Report* as a free download.

OnGuardOnline

www.onguardonline.gov

This website provides great antifraud prevention tips. Its File a Complaint section lets you get information on many different scams, and gives clear information on where to report Internet-related frauds, scams, and suspicious activity.

United States Computer Emergency Readiness Team (US-CERT)

www.us-cert.gov/index.html

The US-CERT website is the go-to place for top-notch information on business security. To stay on top of the latest threats, visit *www.us-cert.gov/cas/bulletins/* to sign up to receive weekly Cyber Security Bulletins, delivered to your inbox.

Protection Software and Utilities

Microsoft Safety & Security

https://www.microsoft.com/security/pc-security/password-checker.aspx?WT.mc_id=Site_Link

This password-checker website lets you test the strength of a password.

Trusteer Rapport

www.trusteer.com

Trusteer Rapport is a web browser add-in that increases anti-phishing protection in most modern web browsers. Trusteer Rapport locks down web browsers, checks to make sure that websites use authentic current digital certificates, blocks drive-by downloads, and helps prevent online fraud.

VIPRE Antivirus Business

www.gfi.com

GFI offers a 30-day trial of VIPRE Antivirus Business. This product provides speedy, low-impact protection against viruses, spyware, rootkits, and other threats.

Security Policy Templates

SANS Information Security Policy Templates

www.sans.org/security-resources/policies/

You can find a wealth of sample security policy templates at this website. The templates are free to use, and can greatly speed up security policy implementation at your organization.

Who to Contact/Where to Complain

If you've received a phishing email, forward it to *spam@uce.gov*. You should also forward it to the organization impersonated in the phishing email. Most organizations have information on their websites about where to report problems.

If you receive suspicious email that includes the name and/or logo of the FDIC, the Patriot Act, or another federal agency and believe it's a scam, report it to the FDIC. You can forward the email to *alert@fdic.gov* or call the FDIC directly at 877-ASK-FDIC.

To report problems with online transactions (between buyer and seller) or office supply scams, contact:

- The FTC, *https://www.ftccomplaintassistant.gov/*
- Your state attorney general, *www.naag.org*
- Your county or state consumer protection agency
- The Better Business Bureau, *http://www.bbb.org/*

Appendix C
References

Acohido, Byron, and Jon Swartz. "Botnet scams are exploding." *USA Today,* March 16, 2008. Accessed February 22, 2011. *www.usatoday.com/tech/news/computersecurity/2008-03-16-computer-botnets_N.htm*

Associated Press. "NJ inmate, 7 Ohio men charged in credit card fraud." *Bloomberg Businessweek,* April 2, 2010. Accessed February 22, 2011. *www.businessweek.com/ap/financialnews/D9EQVHI00.htm*

Bray, Chad, Cassell Bryan-Low, and Siobhan Gorman. "Accounts Raided in Global Bank Hack." WSJ.com, October 1, 2010. Accessed February 28, 2011. *http://online.wsj.com/article/SB10001424052748704483004575523811617488380.html*

Cyber Looting Awareness & Security Project. "What Is Regulation E?". 2011. Accessed February 18, 2011. *http://yourmoneyisnotsafeinthebank.org/RegE.php*

Cyber Looting Awareness & Security Project. *Cybercrime: NO ONE is safe from becoming a victim of cybercrime!* Whitepaper, n.d. Accessed February 28, 2011. *http://yourmoneyisnotsafeinthebank.org/whitepapers/what_is_cybercrime.pdf*

CyberSource. *2011 Online Fraud Report: Online Payment Fraud Trends, Merchant Practices and Benchmarks,* 12th edition. Accessed March 2, 2011. *http://forms.cybersource.com/forms/FraudReport2011NACYBSwww2011*

Damballa. *Top 10 Botnet Threat Report—2010*. Released February 15, 2011. Accessed February 22, 2011. *www.damballa.com/downloads/r_pubs/Damballa_2010_Top_10_Botnets_Report.pdf*

Facebook.com. Accessed February 21, 2011.

"Fake Amazon receipt generator discovered." Help Net Security website, December 7, 2010. Accessed February 18, 2011. *http://www.net-security.org/malware_news.php?id=1556*

Federal Bureau of Investigation (FBI). "2009 Financial Crimes Report: Fiscal Year 2009 (October 1, 2008—September 30, 2009)." n.d. Accessed February 24, 2011. *www.fbi.gov/stats-services/publications/financial-crimes-report-2009*

Federal Trade Commission (FTC). "Spotting an Impostor: Scammers Pose as Friends, Family and Government Agencies." February 2011. Accessed February 28, 2011. *www.ftc.gov/bcp/edu/pubs/consumer/alerts/alt111.shtm*

Ferguson, Aaron J. "Fostering E-Mail Security Awareness: The West Point Carronade." *EDUCAUSE Quarterly*, 28 (1), 2005. Accessed February 28, 2011. *www.educause.edu/EDUCAUSE+Quarterly/EDUCAUSEQuarterlyMagazineVolum/FosteringEMailSecurityAwarenes/157333*

GCG. Steele Settlement website. Updated April 30, 2009. Accessed February 22, 2011. *www.steelesettlement.com/*

Google.com. Accessed February 12, 2011.

Greenspan, Stephen, Dr. *Annals of Gullibility: Why We Get Duped and How to Avoid It.* Westport, CT: Praeger, December 2008.

Guardian Analytics. "Independent Study Reveals Banks Have a New Troubled Asset: Their Customers." Press release, March 9, 2010. Accessed February 18, 2011. *www.guardiananalytics.com/newsandevents/press_03092010.php*

Internet Crime Complaint Center (IC3). "Compromise of User's Online Banking Credentials Targets Commercial Bank Accounts." Intelligence Note, November 3, 2009. Accessed February 17, 2011. *www.ic3.gov/media/2009/091103-1.aspx*

Internet Crime Complaint Center (IC3). "IC3 2009 Annual Report on Internet Crime Released." Press release, March 12, 2010. Accessed February 4, 2011. *www.ic3.gov/media/2010/100312.aspx*

Internet Crime Complaint Center (IC3). "Internet Crime Complaint Center's (IC3) Scam Alerts." December 2, 2010. Accessed February 28, 2011. *www.ic3.gov/media/2010/101202.aspx*

Internet Crime Complaint Center (IC3). 2008 *Internet Crime Report.* March 31, 2009. Accessed February 28, 2011. *www.ic3.gov/media/annualreport/2008_IC3Report.pdf*

Internet Crime Complaint Center (IC3). *2009 Internet Crime Report.* March 12, 2010. Accessed March 6, 2011. *www.ic3.gov/media/annualreport/2009_IC3Report.pdf*

Internet Crime Complaint Center (IC3). *2010 Internet Crime Report.* February 24, 2011. Accessed March 6, 2011. *www.ic3.gov/media/annualreport/2010_IC3Report.pdf*

IP2Location.com. Accessed February 8, 2011.

Kaspersky Lab. "Facebook ranks fourth in the Top 10 most popular phishing targets in the first quarter of 2010." Kaspersky Lab website, May 12, 2010. Accessed February 21, 2011. *www.kaspersky.com/news?id=207576083*

Klein, Amit. "New Financial Trojan Keeps Online Banking Sessions Open After Users 'Logout'." Trusteer blog. February 22, 2011. Accessed February 22, 2011. *www.trusteer.com/blog/new-financial-trojan-keeps-online-banking-sessions-open-after-users-%E2%80%9Clogout%E2%80%9D*

KnowBe4.com. Accessed February 28, 2011.

Landesman, Mary. "Phishing Filters and Toolbar." About.com, 2011. Accessed February 18, 2011. *http://antivirus.about.com/od/freeantivirussoftware/tp/phishingfilter.htm*

Laudon, Kenneth, and Carol Guercio Traver. *E-Commerce 2011.* 7th edition. Upper Saddle River, NJ: Prentice Hall, November 2010.

LinkedIn.com. Accessed February 21, 2011.

Markoff, John. "Larger Prey Are Targets of Phishing." *The New York Times,* April 16, 2008. Accessed February 28, 2011. *www.nytimes.com/2008/04/16/technology/16whale.html*

Maurer, David W. *The Big Con: The Story of the Confidence Man.* Indianapolis, IN: The Bobbs-Merrill Company, 1940.

McGlasson, Linda, ed. "ACH Fraud Sparks Another Suit." BankInfoSecurity.com, June 1, 2010. Accessed February 18, 2011. *www.bankinfosecurity.com/articles.php?art_id=2592*

McMillian, Robert. "Facebook Takes Steps to Deal With Gift Card Scams." *PCWorld,* April 7, 2010. Accessed February 18, 2011. *www.pcworld.com/article/193682/facebook_takes_steps_to_deal_with_gift_card_scams.html*

Miniwatts Marketing Group. "Internet World Users by Language." Updated June 20, 2010. Accessed February 4, 2011. *www.internetworldstats.com/stats7.htm*

"Mortgage Foreclosure Rescue Scams." Fraud Guides website, n.d. Accessed February 20, 2011. *http://www.fraudguides.com/mortgage-foreclosure-rescue-scam.asp*

National Cyber Security Alliance, and Visa Inc. *2010 NCSA / Visa Inc. Small Business Study.* November 30, 2010. Accessed February 28, 2011. *http://www.staysafeonline.org/sites/default/files/resource_documents/2010_Full_Small_Business_Study_FINAL11%2023.pdf*

Navetta, David. "Online Banking and 'Reasonable Security' Under the Law: Breaking New Ground?". Information Law Group website, January 14, 2010. Accessed February 12, 2011. *www.infolawgroup.com/2010/01/articles/reasonable-security/online-banking-and-reasonable-security-under-the-law-breaking-new-ground/*

PandaLabs. "Cyber-crime black market undercovered." PandaLabs blog, January 20, 2011. Accessed February 12, 2011. *http://pandalabs.pandasecurity.com/black-market-undercovered/*

PayPal. Purchase Protection web page, 2011. Accessed February 22, 2011. *https://cms.paypal.com/us/cgi-bin/?cmd=_render-content&content_ID=security/buyer_protection*

PayPal. Seller Protection web page, 2011. Accessed February 22, 2011. *https://cms.paypal.com/us/cgi-bin/?cmd=_render-content&content_ID=security/seller_protection_learn_more*

PCMag.com. "Phishing Effectiveness: 35 Credit Cards in 5 Hours." Security Watch blog, January 28, 2011. Accessed February 4, 2011.
http://blogs.pcmag.com/securitywatch/2011/01/phishing_effectiveness_35_cred.php

Ponemon and Guardian Analytics. "2010 Business Banking Trust Study." Executive summary, March 9, 2010. Accessed February 18, 2011. *www.guardiananalytics.com/newsandevents/press_03092010.php*

RSA. Response to "Worse than Nothing: Want to get phished? Don't worry, it won't hurt" blog entry, September 28, 2009. Accessed February 22, 2011. *http://blog.iangreenleaf.com/2009/07/worse-than-nothing.html*

Schonfeld, Erick. "Fraudsters Drain PayPal Accounts Through iTunes." TechCrunch. com, August 23, 2010. Accessed February 18, 2011. *http://techcrunch.com/2010/08/23/paypal-itunes-fraud/*

Woyke, Elizabeth, and Sonja Ryst. "Someone's Been Using My Gift Card." *Bloomberg Businessweek,* January 15, 2007. Accessed February 18, 2011. *www.businessweek.com/magazine/content/07_03/b4017054.htm*

SpamArrest.com. Accessed February 18, 2011.

Symantec. *Symantec Internet Security Threat Report Trends for 2009.* Volume XV, April 2010. Accessed February 12, 2011. *http://eval.symantec.com/mktginfo/enterprise/white_papers/b-whitepaper_exec_summary_internet_security_threat_report_xv_04-2010.en-us.pdf*

Symantec. *Symantec Report on Rogue Security Software, July 08 – June 09.* October 2009. Accessed February 28, 2011. *http://eval.symantec.com/mktginfo/enterprise/white_papers/b-symc_report_on_rogue_security_software_WP_20100385.en-us.pdf*

TowerGroup. "New Regulatory Changes and Consumer Confidence Are at the Center of the Sales Surge." Press release, November 24, 2010. Accessed February 18, 2011. *www.towergroup.com/research/news/news.htm?newsId=8005500*

Trusteer.com. Accessed February 9, 2011.

Twitter.com. Accessed February 21, 2011.

United States Courts. Subpoena to Appear and Testify at a Hearing or Trial in a Civil Action (form). Revised July 2010. Accessed March 1, 2011. *www.uscourts.gov/uscourts/FormsAndFees/Forms/AO088.pdf*

Weill, Andrew. *The Natural Mind: An Investigation of Drugs and the Higher Consciousness.* Boston: Mariner Books, July 1998.

What's My Pass? "The Top 500 Worst Passwords of All Time." November 30, 2008. Accessed February 15, 2011. *www.whatsmypass.com/the-top-500-worst-passwords-of-all-time*

YouTube.com. Accessed February 21, 2011.

Index

Register at

www.knowbe4.com/free-cyberheist-ebook

to receive a **FREE** ebook version of this book!